AFTER DIVESTITURE:

What the AT&T Settlement Means for Business and Residential Telephone Service

by Samuel A. Simon
written with Michael Whelan

Knowledge Industry Publications, Inc.
White Plains, NY and London

Communications Library

After Divestiture: What the AT&T Settlement Means for Business
and Residential Telephone Service

Library of Congress Cataloging in Publication Data

Simon, Sam, 1945-
  After divestiture.

  (Communications library)
  Bibliography: p.
  Includes index.
  1. American Telephone and Telegraph Company.
2. Telephone--United States.   I. Title.   II. Series.
HE8846.A55S52   1984   384.6'3'0973   84-21301
ISBN 0-86729-110-9

Printed in the United States of America

10 9 8 7 6 5 4 3 2 1

Table of Contents

List of Tables and Figures

iv

LIST OF ACRONYMS

ATTIX   AT&T Interexchange Company

BOC   Bell Operating Company

CALC   Customer Access Line Charge

CSO   Central Services Organization

ENFIA   Exchange Network Facilities for
Interstate Access

IC   Inter-LATA Carrier

LATA   Local Access and Transport Area

MFJ   Modification of Final Judgment

OCC   Other Common Carrier

POP   Point of Presence

SLU   Subscriber Line Usage

Acknowledgments

This book was initially published as a booklet, written soon after the AT&T divestiture was announced. Joseph Waz, Jr. and Paul Stern co-authored that booklet with Samuel A. Simon. Subsequently, a new workbook version was produced with the assistance of a community service grant from Illinois Bell Telephone.

This edition could not have been completed without the assistance of Michael J. Whelan, who helped to research and prepare an initial draft; and without the production and coordination assistance of the entire TRAC staff, especially Lily Ferrone, Page Giffin and Kelly Griffen.

Introduction

On January 1, 1984, the telephone industry in the U.S. as it had developed for over half a century ceased to exist. In the name of increased competition and the consumer, the U.S. Justice Department ended a decade-long antitrust lawsuit by entering into an agreement with AT&T to break up the largest company in the world. Known now as the divestiture of AT&T, there is no adequate way to describe how significant an event the divestiture is for all Americans.

Nor has this significance been lost on typical telephone consumers. Their reaction has increasingly been one of great anger and frustration. They can see few or no benefits to themselves from the divestiture. The old saw, "If it ain't broke, don't fix it," describes the reaction of most residential and small business consumers to the break-up. This public reaction may well be justified. It is difficult to pinpoint any tangible benefit for the residential consumer from divestiture.

On the other hand, the largest telecommunications users, and the equipment and long-distance service competitors to AT&T, are experiencing important benefits. The largest users of telecommunications services were not satisfied with AT&T's technology or service. With the end of the Bell System monopoly, the state-of-the-art technology in switching and other telecommunicating areas is rapidly changing. The simple fact that the new regional companies are no longer required to procure all their needs from Western Electric has widened the market for other manufacturers.

Long-distance companies are preparing to take advantage of their new access to local-exchange markets guaranteed by the divestiture order. The competition generated among the new companies will significantly benefit the small number of very heavy users of long-distance service that account for most of the long-distance revenues. According to AT&T, one-tenth of 1% of the long-distance users account for 19.8% of their revenues. On the other hand, 73% of residential customers spend *less than* $10 a month on

1

long-distance service and 86% of the business customers spend *less than* $50 a month on long-distance. Reduction in long-distance rates can be expected to approach 10% to 30% over the next 5 to 10 years.

But as long-distance rates go down, benefiting the heaviest users of long-distance, upward pressures on local rates will continue. In anticipation of the divestiture, local rates jumped almost 50%, on the average, across the country as the result of rate increase requests filed in 1983. In addition, local telephone company customers are facing the prospect of major monthly surcharges, known as access fees, simply for the right to make long-distance telephone calls.

Divestiture by itself would have been confusing and frustrating enough if it was the only change taking place in the telephone industry. But simultaneously with the divestiture, the Federal Communications Commission (FCC) decided to revamp the way telephone service has been priced in the U.S. over the past 50 years. Repricing of telephone service complicated an already confusing situation. It involved crucial questions of who would pay billions of dollars in costs of local telephone company plant, long-distance customers or local customers. And within those categories, which users would pay the most?

Misconceptions about what the changes are in the telephone industry and what they mean can have a major impact on millions of business and residential consumers. Without good information, many consumers could suffer economic losses. We have identified four different areas in which consumers are at risk because of the confusion caused by divestiture.

1. Consumers risk taking improper action that could result in the loss of service or money. Simply having a representative from the wrong company come to your home or office to look at a problem can cost hundreds of dollars.

2. Consumers risk loss from uninformed or mistaken buying decisions. Purchasing a telephone set or system that does not meet your needs is expensive not only because of the wasted money, but often because of inferior service received from the wrong equipment.

3. Consumers are at risk if they delay decisions that could actually save them money—such as buying their own telephone or subscribing to competitive long-distance carriers when it makes sense to do so. For residential consumers, buying instead of renting could save hundreds of dollars over time. For the business user, the stakes are much higher. Even the smallest businesses may end up spending thousands of dollars needlessly, simply be-

cause they don't understand the strategy dictated by the new telephone environment.

4. Consumers are also at risk from new telephone rip-off artists. Whenever there is a period of dramatic change, confusion and uncertainty, there are people who will try to take advantage of the situation. Telephony is no exception. Even before divestiture was formalized, there was evidence of unscrupulous advertising and marketing practices.

Consumers can best protect themselves if they have access to accurate, understandable information. The purpose of this book is to provide that kind of information. We have written and structured it to be of use to a broad cross-section of consumers, businesses, academics, writers—anyone with an interest in or a need to understand the basics behind the changes in the telephone industry.

To achieve this understanding of the industry's new structure, it is necessary first to go over how the system worked before divestiture. Behind the facade of a seemingly simple, integrated telephone network dominated by AT&T was in fact a complex set of corporate and financial relationships.

The first part of this book provides an explanation of the system before divestiture. We then take the reader through the details of the terms and conditions of the divestiture agreement. But divestiture is only one part of the rapidly changing telecommunications environment. A major section of this book is devoted to the changes associated with the repricing of telephone service. Finally, we give some important tips and perspectives on living and working in the postdivestiture telecommunications world.

Unless otherwise noted the author is the source of the figures and tables that appear in this book.

1

The U.S. Telecommunications Industry and the Pressures for Change

A TRADITION OF REGULATED MONOPOLY

When the Communications Act of 1934 was written, telephone service was, in effect, a monopoly provided by one company, American Telephone and Telegraph, and some independent companies that had monopoly rights to local telephone service in the communities they served. The limits of telecommunications technology were largely responsible for allowing the idea of monopoly service; it was just not feasible to have wires from competing companies crowding city streets while failing to provide a single, unified telephone system to the public. But because the public could not shop elsewhere for telephone service, state and federal regulators took pains to develop extensive regulations to protect the public interest.

The 1934 Communications Act

In 1934, Congress passed the Communications Act, the first comprehensive U.S. legislation to establish a regulatory system for national telecommunications, including telephone service. The 1934 act set forth the goal of universal service: that high-quality telephone service should be available to all Americans at a reasonable cost. Fifty years later, the U.S. telecommunications system has 200 million lines, is the backbone of our commercial system and serves 93% of all U.S. households.

5

The FCC

The act also established the FCC and transferred federal regulation of all interstate and foreign wire and radio communications to this commission. It requires that prices be just, reasonable and not unduly discriminatory.

All common carriers (companies that offer communications services to the public) that provide interstate service (crossing state lines) are regulated by the FCC. Interstate services include long-distance service. The commission sets all rates for interstate services and also regulates certain relationships between interstate common carriers (which now include not only AT&T but also its new competitors such as MCI, GTE-Sprint, ITT and Western Union) and local phone companies.

PUCs

All intrastate (within a state) phone services are the responsibility of state public utility or public service commissions, known in the industry as PUCs. They function similarly to the FCC but independently of it. Facets of intrastate phone business regulated by the PUCs include local calling rates, fees for phone equipment, installation charges and all toll (long-distance) calls within the state.

Separations and Settlements

The Federal/State Joint Board, an entity made up of FCC commissioners and representatives of the state PUCs, regulates the process by which long-distance companies pay local phone companies for the right to hook into the local phone network. This process is known as separations and settlements and is discussed more fully in Chapter 3.

Rate of Return

Both state and federal regulation of phone services is based on allowing the regulated company a rate of return on its investment. The public has an interest in financially healthy phone companies that can provide and maintain quality service; companies with a healthy rate of return can attract investors who provide the capital necessary for such service. The public also has an interest in assuring that the rates it pays for phone services are reasonable, since alternative services, especially at the local level, are not generally available. Regulatory bodies must take these twin goals into account in setting rates of return for common carriers.

Rate of return is generally expressed as a percentage of the company's capital investment in a location, i.e., how much money it puts into plant and equipment. Thus, if the FCC grants AT&T a 13% rate of return for long-distance service, that means that AT&T can set its charges (also called its tariff) to bring a 13% profit on every dollar invested. Under this system, the phone company made heavy capital investments, which add to the rate base (the capital base on which its rate of return is calculated).

THE PRESSURES FOR CHANGE

Forces of Technology and Competition

In recent years, rapid technological innovation, such as the development of microwave telecommunications and the blurring of the distinction between telecommunications and computer services, have led to challenges of many long-standing assumptions about the necessity and validity of maintaining monopoly rights. The strong American tradition of competition fueled these fires of change. That spirit quickly recognized the competitive applications of new technologies and steadily increased the pressure to open up the industry.

These pressures for change have been funneled through government bodies that have a say about how much and in what way the telecommunications industry is regulated. Sometimes their involvement has been a matter of overlapping, if not competing, jurisdictions. That is, while Congress set up the FCC as the official body to monitor the industry, there has always been an overlapping of oversight among the FCC, Congress and the Justice Department.

Congress, the most responsive of these bodies to political pressure, has always had the option of revising the Communications Act and has made several, so far unsuccessful, attempts to do so.

The FCC, at first cautious about allowing competition in any form, has gradually become something of a standard-bearer for the cause. Since the late 1960s it has issued more and more rulings opening up the long-distance service and telephone equipment markets to non–AT&T companies.

The Justice Department has been the longest-standing government body to challenge monopoly rights in the telephone industry. As early as 1949, via its authority to enforce the Sherman Antitrust Act, it brought suit alleging that AT&T's structure and business practices stifled competition in the telecommunications equipment industry.

Battles in the Equipment Arena: Carterfone to Computer Inquiry II

Telephone equipment encompasses everything from the home telephone to wiring to sophisticated electronic switching and transmitting facilities. AT&T's Western Electric has been the major manufacturer of such equipment (researched and developed by AT&T's Bell Labs). In 1982 the Bell System bought four fifths of its equipment from Western, whose own 1982 sales were $12.6 billion (nine tenths of which came from Ma Bell). As the single most dominant force in the equipment industry, Western and its captive market in AT&T have long been the object of Justice Department scrutiny (discussed in more detail on page 12).

Carterfone

From the very beginning, AT&T refused to allow non-Bell equipment to be connected into its network, claiming that such equipment would undermine the integrity of the network. One of the first significant challenges to this Bell prohibition came from the Carterfone Co., which in the mid-1960s began to market intercom equipment that could be hooked into its customers' Bell-owned telephone systems (e.g., switchboards and telephones). In 1968, Carterfone won an FCC decision that the telephone company's blanket prohibition against attaching customer-provided terminal equipment was unreasonable, discriminatory and unlawful. The FCC declared that telephone companies could set up reasonable standards for interconnection to ensure the integrity of their network by requiring use of devices known as Protective Connecting Arrangements (PCAs). The decision opened the door to a wave of non-Bell interconnect equipment—everything from sophisticated PBXs (private branch exchanges—i.e., switchboards) to telephone answering machines.

FCC Registration Program

In 1977 the FCC eliminated the PCA requirement and replaced it with its Registration Program. Thereafter, any terminal equipment registered with the FCC could be connected to the telephone network without a connecting device. Among other things, this ruling flooded the market with non-Bell phones available in retail stores. This was the first time customers had the real—and legal—option of owning their own phones instead of leasing one from AT&T.

Computer Inquiry II

An even more significant FCC decision, because it foreshadowed the 1982 divestiture settlement, was Computer Inquiry II in 1980, referred to in the industry as CI-2.

As competition in equipment and electronic service markets developed, the FCC was faced with the question of what terms and conditions should apply to AT&T's involvement in competitive markets. Should AT&T be required to compete under the same regulatory restraints it always had; e.g., approval of rates? Could AT&T compete in markets where its competitors could lower prices without approval while AT&T would be required to get such approval? If AT&T were to be allowed to compete without regulation, how could the FCC be sure that AT&T would not underprice its competitive services and overprice its monopoly services? The potential of cross-subsidization, that is, using revenues from one service (monopoly) to help cut the costs of other services (competitive) was a matter of grave concern to the FCC and Congress.

AT&T was also interested in entering new markets. Since 1956 it had been prohibited from entering any business other than regulated telecommunications services by virtue of the consent decree that settled the Justice Department's 1949 antitrust suit. (See page 13 for more details on the 1956 Consent Decree.)

The FCC undertook to decide these issues in a proceeding known as Computer Inquiry II, named such because it involved deciding whether AT&T could enter the computer business, as well as how AT&T would compete in new markets. In its landmark decision in CI-2, the FCC decided that it would deregulate or detariff all competitive services offered by AT&T—in effect removing FCC controls on rates for such services and equipment. Deregulation applied initially to 1) all customer premises equipment (CPE), e.g. telephones, switches and accessories; 2) new computer-related services, including data transmission and new custom-calling features; and 3) any new service entered into that had been prohibited by the 1956 consent decree. The FCC also said that it would consider deregulation of other services as competition warranted.

To avoid the cross-subsidy problem, the FCC required AT&T to offer all of its deregulated competitive services through a newly formed company—known as a fully separated subsidiary—that would operate at arm's length from the regulated divisions of AT&T. On January 1, 1983, AT&T established such a marketing arm, and named it American Bell. (That name was changed to AT&T Information Systems—ATTIS, since AT&T had to surrender use of the Bell name, except for Bell Labs and overseas operations, after divestiture.) American Bell began life with $350 million in assets transferred from the corporate parent and 29,000 employees, more than 3700 of whom came from Bell Labs. This arm's length arrangement ordered by the FCC was less radical than the 1982 divestiture settlement.

Battles in the Long-Distance Arena:
MCI and the Emergence of the OCCs

The introduction of radar in World War II and its application in microwave radio transmission made it feasible to use such a medium as an alternative to the traditional hard-wire telephone lines, especially in covering long distances. While this application was not immediately recognized as a viable possibility, it did implicitly question the notion that monopoly made sense in long-distance markets, since with microwave many companies could simultaneously transmit over the same corridor between two cities without interfering with one another, and without incurring the tremendous capital costs of laying thousands of miles of wires.

The first company to test the regulatory waters in this area was MCI (then Microwave Communications Inc.), which in 1969 applied for FCC permission to operate a microwave long-distance service between St. Louis and Chicago. The FCC granted permission, not realizing at the time that it would eventually result in widespread competition in long-distance telephone services. Within a few years MCI had developed a long-distance network capable of connecting into telephones in local networks, thus offering a direct challenge to AT&T's Long Lines. In 1975, the FCC in response to a complaint by AT&T, barred the service, which MCI called Execunet. A federal appeals court overturned the FCC ban and ordered Bell to offer connections into its local phone systems to MCI's long-distance facilities. In

1978 the Supreme Court refused to review the appeals court ruling on the ban. In effect, this opened the intercity long-distance market to competition.

Quickly joining MCI in this market was Southern Pacific, which offered Sprint service (now known as GTE-Sprint, since Southern Pacific sold the service to GTE), as well as ITT, Western Union and later Satellite Business Systems (SBS). As a group, these five companies have come to be known as the Other Common Carriers (OCCs), to distinguish them from AT&T. By 1983 the combined revenues of these carriers accounted for 6% of the long-distance market, but their impact on competition in the industry at large has been far greater than their market share indicates.

LEGISLATIVE ATTEMPTS AT REFORM

Along with competitive pressure exerted through the FCC and the appeals courts to open equipment and long-distance markets, there have been recurrent attempts in Congress to revise the Communications Act of 1934, which has become increasingly dated with the emergence of technological innovation (hardly envisioned when the act was written).

Ironically, the first legislative attention came not as the result of pressure from competitors, but as the result of AT&T's reaction to the growing competition. In 1976, the Consumer Communications Reform Act (CCRA) was introduced in both the House and Senate. The bill, which was drafted with the help of AT&T and designed to give legal standing to the Bell System monopoly, quickly picked up the short title of the Bell Bill. The CCRA called for specific tests for competitors to be able to enter the long-distance and terminal-equipment markets. Bell argued that such safeguards were essential to assure the continuance of universal service. The theme of the AT&T lobbying campaign also became the theme of its national advertising campaign, the need for a single national telephone system, or, in advertising parlance, "The System is the Solution." Although the CCRA had more than 200 sponsors at the outset, it died in committee in both houses.

It was re-introduced in both houses in 1979, but by then a pro-competition reaction was setting in. Although the bills died again in committee, Congressional subcommittees began hearings on the need for change in national telecommunications policy. The House Subcommittee on Telecommunications, then chaired by Representative Lionel Van Deerlin (D-CA), undertook the most comprehensive review, which resulted in a proposed total rewrite of the Communications Act of 1934. H. R. 3333 was Van Deerlin's first version, which was then revised into a more limited bill, H. R. 6121.

In the Senate, two bills were introduced, S. 611 and S. 622. None of the bills moved out of committee that year.

In 1979, the mood of Congress was just the opposite of what AT&T originally wanted with its Bell Bill in 1976. By 1980, the thrust of the legislation was to promote competition by limiting AT&T's ability to cross-subsidize its equipment and long-distance services. At the same time that the FCC was involved in its CI-2 proceeding, legislation in Congress was also calling for fully separated subsidiaries within AT&T for competitive services.

In 1980, the House efforts were stalled in committee again. The Senate merged S. 611 and S. 622 into a single bill, S. 2872, which also died at the end of the Congressional session.

The 1980 elections brought about a change in House subcommittee chairmanship that had an important impact on the tone of the House legislative efforts. Congressman Van Deerlin lost his re-election bid, and Timothy Wirth (D-CO) took over the chairmanship of the House Subcommittee on Telecommunications. Wirth had been a vocal critic of Van Deerlin's earlier efforts, claiming that the bills had not gone far enough to assure full and fair competition by restricting AT&T.

In 1981, Wirth introduced a brand-new bill, H. R. 5158, which called for stringent separations in AT&T's structures to assure that AT&T could not subsidize its competitive efforts from monopoly revenues. But Wirth's legislative efforts were overtaken by the announcement of the settlement of the Justice Department antitrust action and the proposed divestiture on January 8, 1982.

Wirth quickly revised his bill to be compatible with the divestiture and continued his push for enactment. His subcommittee passed the bill, but it died in the full Energy and Commerce Committee under the weight of a massive lobbying effort by AT&T.

Congress stepped back during the remainder of 1982, refusing to commit itself on the divestiture. With the announcement by the FCC in July 1983 of a repricing plan that threatened to add significant costs to local telephone bills, legislation was launched again in both the House and the Senate. This legislation is discussed in detail in Chapter 6.

THREE DECADES OF
JUSTICE DEPARTMENT ANTITRUST ACTION

In the end, it was neither the FCC nor Congress, but the Justice Department, that precipitated the most dramatic restructuring of the industry. It began with a series of antitrust actions started in 1949 and culminating in the 1982 Consent Decree, which required the breakup of AT&T.

The Justice Department's Antitrust Division, whose objective is to remove roadblocks to competition in industry, contended that AT&T was standing in the way of increased competition in various aspects of phone service. In 1949, the Justice Department brought suit in New Jersey federal court, seeking to split off Western Electric, AT&T's manufacturing arm, on the grounds that it was freezing out competitors from selling phone equipment compatible with the Bell System.

In 1956, Justice and AT&T agreed to a consent decree, which gave the Antitrust Division some but not all of the changes it was looking for. The decree limited AT&T's business activities to furnishing common-carrier communications services (services and facilities whose charges are subject to regulation under the 1934 Communications Act). AT&T also had to license patents for its technology to competitors. Although the agreement left AT&T intact, its effect was to lock AT&T out of new, nonregulated areas like data processing and computer services, which have undergone enormous growth in the last two decades. And although none of the parties to settlement realized it at the time, the 1956 consent decree turned out to be a significant factor in the eventual breakup of AT&T a quarter of a century later.

Developments following the 1956 consent decree convinced the Justice Department that the decree's restrictions were still not preventing anticompetitive behavior, especially in CPE markets (phones and associated equipment used in homes and businesses). The Justice Department also felt AT&T was standing in the way of competition in long-distance phone service from the OCCs.

So in 1974 the department brought another antitrust suit against AT&T in the Federal District Court in Washington, D.C., and once again called for the divestiture of Western Electric (the manufacturing arm). The Department later revised its request and sought to break off the operating companies in a way which would separate the local exchange functions (local dialtone and switching services) from AT&T's other functions, including long-distance service and manufacturing phone equipment.

The suit dragged on for years and did not come to trial until 1981. Delays were attributable in large part to the hard line taken by AT&T, which spent $300 million in defense, sending 70 attorneys to make court appearances and employing hundreds more to work on the case behind the scenes.

For years, AT&T argued primarily that break-up—the divestiture of the operating companies—would damage the national defense and ultimately destroy a uniform, quality telephone system throughout the U.S. But the Justice Department remained adamant in its prosecution of the case. As late as the fall of 1981, Assistant Attorney General William Baxter vowed to litigate "to the eyeballs."

Twice during the trial, the Justice Department initiated settlement negotiations with AT&T, but both efforts failed. Finally, on December 31, 1981, the Justice Department and AT&T reported that they had resumed negotiations, and on January 8, 1982, the parties announced that they had reached a settlement, the now-famous divestiture agreement. It is treated in detail in Chapter 4, but to appreciate the enormous scope of the settlement, it is necessary first to understand the prior structure and operations of AT&T and the telecommunications industry.

2

The Telecommunications Industry Before Divestiture

THE MAJOR PLAYERS

AT&T: Its Corporate Structure

The divestiture agreement split up the largest company in the world, with assets of $155 billion and one million employees. Prior to divestiture, AT&T's operations could be grouped into three broad categories, identified by its major subsidiaries, as shown in Figure 2.1.

1. The 22 BOCs. These were the local telephone companies that had the most direct business dealings with the local consumer. They handled 80% of the nation's local telephone service business. They included such familiar names as Southwestern Bell, Southern Bell, New York Telephone and Illinois Bell. The BOCs provided local telephone service, installations and repairs within the communities they served, including connection into and out of the local and long-distance networks used by their subscribers. In addition, they operated their own long-distance networks, which carried all Bell System calls made within the states they served. The BOCs were regulated by PUCs, which oversaw all intrastate service.

2. AT&T Long Lines. This was the interstate long-distance division (called AT&T Communications since divestiture). It carried all Bell System calls made between states. The Long Lines division was regulated by the FCC and its revenues were separate from the BOC revenues.

Figure 2.1: Structure by Function of AT&T Key Subsidiaries, Before Divestiture

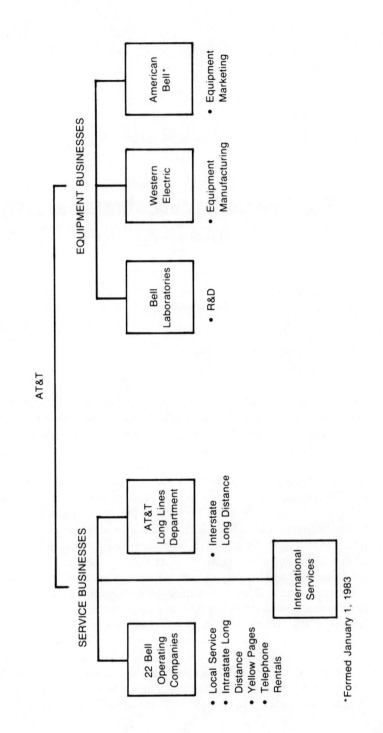

AT&T

EQUIPMENT BUSINESSES

Bell Laboratories
- R&D

Western Electric
- Equipment Manufacturing

American Bell*
- Equipment Marketing

SERVICE BUSINESSES

22 Bell Operating Companies
- Local Service
- Intrastate Long Distance
- Yellow Pages
- Telephone Rentals

AT&T Long Lines Department
- Interstate Long Distance

International Services

*Formed January 1, 1983

3. Western Electric, Bell Labs and American Bell. These companies operated in the equipment end of AT&T's business.

Western Electric, whose 1982 sales were $12.6 billion, was AT&T's manufacturer of telephone equipment (everything from telephones to switching and transmission equipment). The Bell System (BOCs and Long Lines) bought four fifths of its equipment from Western; these transactions accounted for 90% of Western's revenues. Western Electric was dismantled after divestiture, with its functions divided among several of the new divisions of AT&T.

Bell Laboratories, famous for innovations such as the transistor, was AT&T's research-and-development arm. Western Electric supplied 52% of its budget. One percent of BOC's revenues also went to Bell Labs, and, combined with Western Electric's contributions, these funds accounted for an additional 44% of Bell Labs' budget. Part of Bell Labs went to the BOCs after divestiture. What remained was renamed AT&T Bell Labs.

American Bell, officially renamed ATTIS after divestiture, was the new division created on January 1, 1983, as a result of the FCC's CI-2. Its function was to design and market CPE manufactured primarily by Western.

All these companies were subsidiaries of American Telephone and Telegraph, whose chairman, Charles Brown, oversaw this empire from its famous headquarters at 195 Broadway in New York City (which also changed when AT&T moved to 550 Madison Ave. in Manhattan). On January 1, 1984, the old building at 195 Broadway was given to a new corporate foundation. While the official company name was always AT&T, the name Bell has been used interchangeably with it, and the term Bell System along with the well-known Bell System logo have been used to identify its combined local and long-distance networks.

The Independent Telephone Companies

In addition to the 22 BOCs, there are about 1450 other local phone companies, unaffiliated with Bell and known as the independents. They range in size from General Telephone and Electric Co. (GTE), whose $22 billion in assets include those of substantial manufacturing operations to very small independents with revenues only in the hundreds of thousands of dollars. In the area they serve, they conduct local service monopolies just as the BOCs do. To provide their customers access to long-distance service outside their exchanges, the independents' systems connect into the AT&T intrastate and interstate networks. As a group they account for about 20% of U.S. telephone customers, although they cover 44% of the country geographically. They also have a higher concentration of rural and residence customers than the Bell system.

The Long-Distance Competitors (OCCs)

These are the Other Common Carriers, companies licensed by the FCC to provide interstate service in competition with the Bell System. The largest of these are MCI, GTE-Sprint, ITT, Western Union and SBS. They own and operate their own microwave and/or satellite networks that connect into the local BOC and independent exchanges, so that OCC subscribers can use the same phones as they do for AT&T calls. The method used in carrying OCC calls is essentially the same as that used for AT&T interexchange (long-distance) calls, except that the intercity portion of the OCC call goes over the OCC network instead of over the AT&T network.

The same system applies for AT&T long-distance calls except that such calls go from the local phone company exchange to an AT&T long-distance terminal, where they are transmitted to a distant AT&T receiving terminal. In the case of AT&T, such calls often go over "hard-wire" lines rather than satellite or microwave equipment, which were not available when much of the AT&T system was constructed.

LOCAL VS. LONG DISTANCE:
SORTING OUT COSTS AND REVENUES

All long-distance calls, whether intrastate or interstate, from AT&T Long Lines or OCCs, originate and terminate within local telephone exchanges. It is therefore necessary for BOCs to determine what part of the cost of local operations should be allocated to handling long-distance calls that go through their system. To determine and distribute such costs, complex systems have been developed over time, some for dealings between AT&T Long Lines and the operating companies, some for dealings between the Bell System and the independents and some for dealings between AT&T and the OCCs. These methods, which are shown in Figure 2.2 include the following: separations, division of revenues, settlements and Exchange Networks Facilities for Interstate Access (ENFIA) tariffs.

Figure 2.2: Sorting Out Long-Distance Costs and Revenues between Local Companies and Long-Distance Carriers

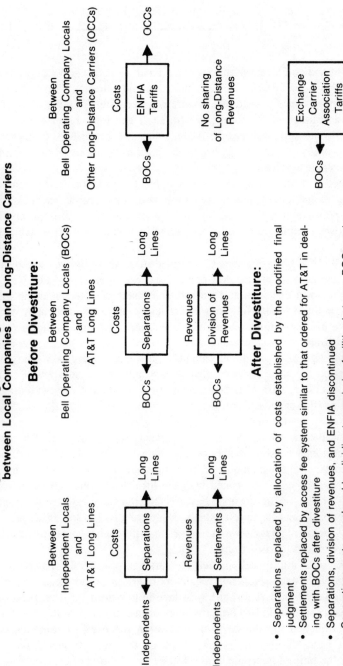

Before Divestiture:

Between
Independent Locals
and
AT&T Long Lines

Between
Bell Operating Company Locals (BOCs)
and
AT&T Long Lines

Between
Bell Operating Company Locals
and
Other Long-Distance Carriers (OCCs)

After Divestiture:

- Separations replaced by allocation of costs established by the modified final judgment
- Settlements replaced by access fee system similar to that ordered for AT&T in dealing with BOCs after divestiture
- Separations, division of revenues, and ENFIA discontinued
- Separations system replaced by dividing transmission facilities between BOCs and AT&T (previously jointly owned)
- Division of Revenues replaced by access fee to be paid by AT&T
- ENFIA replaced by access fee to be paid by OCCs

Separations

The plant and equipment used to provide local telephone service was also used to carry long-distance traffic—interstate and intrastate. In the early years of long-distance service, when there was very little long-distance calling, common usage of the local plant for local and long-distance was not considered important. But as time passed, the question of how to allocate the cost of jointly and commonly used local plant became central to the pricing of telephone service.

The process of allocating plant and equipment, and the associated costs, between local and long-distance service was known as separations. Initially, the local phone companies bore the burden of the local exchange costs, since the overwhelming amount of use of the local lines was attributable to local calls.

But in 1930 the U.S. Supreme Court ruled in *Smith v. Illinois* that in order to set intrastate rates, the cost of the local exchange should be divided between intrastate and interstate operations. Changes were not made immediately on the federal level, but some states began to take action. A variety of different separations plans evolved and the need for a uniform plan became apparent.

In coming up with a plan to allocate costs, it was relatively easy to distinguish costs on the basis of usage, that is, the number and duration of each category of service, intrastate, interstate or local. Costs that vary with usage are called traffic-sensitive costs.

But certain plant facilities were not traffic-sensitive. These facilities, referred to as the local loop, were the equipment, wires and poles that connected a customer's phone to the local exchange central office. It cost the phone company the same amount to maintain these whether they were used or not. Thus, the costs associated with the local loop were referred to as fixed costs or non–traffic-sensitive costs (NTS). But the local loop was used jointly for local calls, state toll calls and interstate calls. The challenge to state and federal regulators was to come up with a plan to allocate these costs to appropriate jurisdictions.

In 1942, following allegations that the earnings of AT&T's Long Lines Department were excessive, state regulators requested a more equitable division of toll revenues. A formula was devised to determine what percentage of local costs should be borne by long-distance users. Initially, the formula was designed to allocate costs strictly on the basis of usage called Subscriber Line Usage (SLU). The allocation to interstate would be expressed as the ratio of interstate usage (SLU) to total usage of the local loop:

$$\frac{\text{Interstate Usage (SLU)}}{\text{Total Usage (Local, Interstate and Intrastate)}}$$

After World War II the cost of local service began to rise at a greater rate than long-distance service, mainly because technological innovations such as microwave made long-distance more economical to operate. Therefore, in order to keep local rates low—the goal of universal telephone service—the regulatory agencies gradually began to shift a larger share of the fixed local loop costs onto interstate (Long Lines Department) operations.

This shift was achieved by gradually multiplying the SLU portion of the formula by a weighted factor. The idea was introduced in 1952 as the Charleston Plan. The effect of the plan was to allocate nearly twice as much non–traffic-sensitive plant costs to interstate as would be assigned on a straight usage or SLU basis. The new factor came to be known as the Subscriber Plant Factor (SPF). Thus, the formula for allocating between long-distance and local became:

$$\frac{\text{Interstate Usage (SLU)} \times \text{Plant Factor (SPF)}}{\text{Total Local Exchange Usage}}$$

In 1980, the plant factor (SPF) was about 3.3 times the usage factor (SLU) for the Bell System as a whole. The result was that about 25% of the local loop costs were assigned to Long Lines. The costs amounted to about 37% of Long Lines revenues.

It is now widely agreed that such an allocation of costs favors local service at the expense of long-distance. The emergence of competition has made this imbalance a major issue in repricing telecommunications. It has led to the current battle over access fees (discussed in Chapter 6).

The separation formula is set by a group of state PUC regulators and FCC commissioners acting together in the Joint Board. The Joint Board has also taken the position that the separation formula favors the BOCs too heavily at the expense of the long-distance user. In 1982 the Joint Board formally froze the SPF factor at its current 3.3 level and began consideration of a process to reduce the SPF factor. A reduction in the SPF factor would reduce the amount of money collected by the BOCs from the long-distance companies.

But in April 1983, in response to the divestiture, the Joint Board met in Washington and decided that it would freeze the entire separations formula for two years, pending the complete implementation of divestiture. Thus the total amount of money flowing between interstate long-distance markets and the BOCs will not be decreased before April 1985.

The method of collection of these revenues described below as the division of revenues process has changed. It has been replaced by an access fee method of collection, described in Chapter 6. And the FCC access fee decision, also described in Chapter 6, will (if it is not overturned by Congress) require the BOCs to collect a portion of the long-distance revenue as a flat monthly surcharge on the local customer bill, instead of as part of the per-minute charge collected from the long-distance customer.

Division of Revenues

This was the next step in the process of transferring revenues between long-distance and local markets in the predivestiture environment. Division of revenues (DR) was a financial transaction between AT&T and its BOCs that took place after separations, the process used to determine the formula for allocation of costs between AT&T and the BOCs. DR was the process of payment to recover those costs—both SLU and SPF. Since long-distance calling was billed on the local bill and collected by the BOC, the transition usually involved payment by the BOC to AT&T Long Lines. But certain high-cost areas did not recover their full long-distance costs from the long-distance customers in their area of service, and therefore received payments from AT&T Long Lines.

The Division of Revenues system is coming to an end, since there is no longer a single company to divide its revenue among its various parts. Instead, it is being replaced by a new system of access charges collected by the BOCs from all long-distance companies. As mentioned, the amount to be collected—the amount that the BOCs are entitled to collect via the separations process described above—will not change immediately.

Settlements

This procedure was the same as Division of Revenues, except that it applied to Bell's dealings with independent telephone companies. Historically, AT&T Long Lines carried interstate long-distance traffic into and out of the local exchange markets served by the independent telephone companies, such as GTE and Continental Telephones, just as it had for its own Bell companies. With the arrival of competition, the OCCs also interconnected with these independent companies to pay the interconnection under the Exchange Network Facilities for Interstate Access (ENFIA) tariff.

The method of payment by the independent companies to AT&T for carrying its interstate long distance traffic, and the payment by AT&T to the independent companies for accepting interstate long-distance calls from its markets, is accomplished through the settlements procedure. It involves applying the separations formula to the interstate long-distance revenues associated with the independent companies' local exchanges.

In addition to the settlement of interstate long-distance revenues, independent companies also had to arrange for payments to BOCs for carrying their intrastate traffic. This process, similar to settlements, was called compensation.

After divestiture, the settlements procedure and the compensation procedure, like the DR system, were replaced by a new system of access charges. But independent telephone companies have to arrange for having their calls transferred into, out of and through adjacent BOC exchanges. Indeed, for a call to be carried from one part of an independent company exchange to another, it must travel through a BOC exchange. Payments for this type of service are negotiated directly between the independents and the BOCs and continue to be referred to as compensation.

ENFIA

The OCCs—the other common carriers—(MCI, GTE-Sprint, etc.) interconnect with the BOCs and must also pay for the cost of exchange services. The charge, referred to as an ENFIA tariff, was set in 1979 by the FCC in a highly contested proceeding. The ENFIA tariff provided that the OCCs pay less than AT&T Long Lines did for accessing the BOC exchange under the Division of Revenue process. The reason for the difference in payment level was the different quality and type of connection provided by the BOCs to the OCCs compared to that provided to AT&T Long Lines. AT&T contended that the differential was far too large compared to what it had to pay, while the OCCs argued that they paid far too much in light of their inferior connections. Consumers experienced the difference as the need to dial up to 24 different digits to complete a call through an OCC compared to 10 digits (area code and number) for AT&T.

After divestiture this ENFIA tariff procedure was replaced with a new tariff that charges all common carriers, including AT&T, on an equal basis—once access conections became equal. (See Chapter 5 for a discussion of equal access.) Under the FCC access fee decision (discussed in detail in Chapter 6), the difference between what the OCCs (what had been

ENFIA) and AT&T (what had been Division of Revenues) pay to the BOCs is reduced until equal access is achieved and equal payments apply (a process that will take up to three years).

The level of the ENFIA tariff had been one of the most controversial aspects of competitive telecommunications. The OCCs asserted that AT&T had used the ENFIA tariff to continue alleged anticompetitive practices. AT&T contended that the OCCs paid much less than their fair share of the BOC costs and were unfairly favored by the FCC. What follows is the cost history of the ENFIA tariff up until the divestiture.

ENFIA I $ 98 per line   April 1978 Initial Tariff

ENFIA II $155 per line   When OCC annual revenues are $100 million

ENFIA III $200 per line   When OCC revenues are $250 million

OCC revenues had surpassed the ENFIA III level by December 1982 when the FCC issued its first access fee decision. Initially, the FCC proposed to increase the per-line fee paid by the OCCs to $425, more than a 100% increase. The FCC's April 1984 decision, after reconsidering its earlier proposal, increased the cost to $212.11 per line. And in the Fall of 1984, the BOCs, through their National Exchange Carrier Association, asked the FCC to increase that rate to $230.85 per line.

The AT&T per-line charge is claimed by AT&T to be $700 per line. The OCCs dispute the AT&T figure, claiming that AT&T has paid less. Since AT&T did not pay on a per-line charge (they used Division of Revenues), it has been hard to determine precise figures.

3

The Divestiture Agreement

On January 8, 1982, the world was stunned by the unexpected announcement that the Justice Department and AT&T had reached a settlement of the highly publicized, eight-year-old antitrust suit that called for the dissolution of the AT&T Bell Telephone System.

Before it could become effective, the agreement on settlement required approval by a federal court, a process that wound up taking eight months to achieve. Indeed, the events involved in the approval procedure became as complex as the actual implementation of divestiture would be, once the approval was received.

Immediately there arose a question about which federal court had the authority to approve the agreement. At first, neither AT&T nor the Justice Department treated the agreement as a settlement of the 1974 antitrust suit out of which it came. Rather, they considered their agreement to be a modification of an earlier agreement (consent decree) reached in 1956, which settled a 1949 Justice Department antitrust suit against the company. (That was the 1956 consent decree which, among other things, prohibited AT&T from entering nonregulated businesses like data processing.) Thus, the Justice Department and AT&T first sent their January 8 agreement to a federal district court judge in New Jersey, who technically had jurisdiction over the 1956 consent decree. The New Jersey judge immediately approved the agreement.

This raised concern among policy makers and Federal District Court Judge Harold Greene of the Washington, D.C. District Court that a power play was in the works to bypass the jurisdiction of Judge Greene's court, where the 1974 antitrust case had been in trial. Judge Greene protested and the entire matter was transferred to his court.

25

He then issued an order on January 21 that began public comment proceedings, known as Tunney Act Proceedings, after the federal law that mandates them. These required Greene to receive public comment on the terms of the agreement and to hold public hearings on it.

But even Judge Greene's order to initiate Tunney Act Proceedings generated considerable criticism that the agreement was too vague and not substantial enough for the judge to approve or disapprove. The agreement was only 14 pages long and it called for AT&T to divest itself of its 22 local telephone companies—the Bell Operating Companies BOCs.

But it did not specify *how* that was to be done. Instead, it merely stipulated that AT&T was to develop a plan for reorganization, due within six months after AT&T and the Justice Department received court approval of the agreement. The timetable also stipulated that divestiture was to be completed within 12 months after the plan, in turn, received court approval. Critics expressed concern that such a timetable was inadequate to assure meaningful public input.

Nevertheless, Judge Greene began the hearing process by publishing the original agreement in the *Federal Register*. The process led to major changes in the terms of the original agreement.

TERMS OF THE ORIGINAL AGREEMENT

The original agreement between the Justice Department and AT&T called for the following:

- The 22 BOCs were to be grouped into not less than seven new corporations. These companies would be permitted to offer only local telephone service (also called dial tone, switched services and exchange services). They would no longer be allowed to sell telephone equipment or run Yellow Pages operations.

- A new centralized organization would be formed (later dubbed the Central Services Organization [CSO] to provide centralized technical and management services to the BOCs. It would also serve as a central point of contact for coordinating BOCs for national emergencies and national defense.

- AT&T would keep all its other subsidiaries, notably AT&T Long

Lines (long-distance service), Western Electric (its manufacturing arm), and Bell Laboratories (its research facility).

• From the BOCs, AT&T would assume all intrastate operations except for those within the BOCs' exchange areas. AT&T would also assume ownership of the Yellow Pages directory publications and all Customer Premises Equipment (CPE) leased to Bell System customers.

• All BOCs would provide equal access to their exchanges to all long-distance companies. AT&T would no longer receive favored treatment or favored access.

• AT&T would be freed from restriction in the 1956 Consent Decree, which kept it from entering new communications and computer markets.

Reactions to the Original Agreement

The original agreement left most of the details to be worked out later, when the Plan of Reorganization was submitted. Initial reaction to the agreement in Congressional testimony and later submissions to Judge Greene focused on whether the agreement adequately protected the viability of the local telephone companies.

Some suggested that the agreement was highly advantageous to AT&T, pointing out that AT&T would be shedding its capital-intensive local operating companies, which were locked into limited telephone service offerings. These observers also pointed out that AT&T would take with it its most lucrative markets (notably long-distance service) *plus* a new freedom to compete in the highly lucrative computer and communications markets.

State PUCs and consumer groups expressed concern over the fate of the 22 BOCs after divestiture. They pointed out that the quality and affordability of local service—the universal service ideal—depended on financially healthy local operating companies with adequate capital and lines of business, such as Yellow Pages—a $4 billion annual operation—which the BOCs were to lose after divestiture.

Other issues also arose, especially the question of who would get the valuable Bell name and logo, and who would have access to patents that had been and were being developed by Bell Labs up to the time of divestiture.

Figure 3.1: AT&T After Divestiture

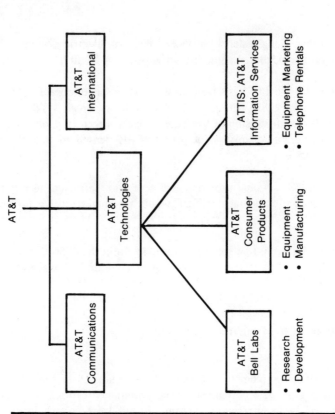
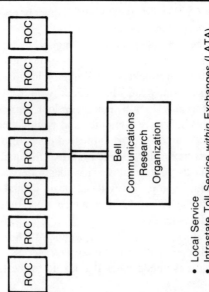

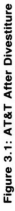

AT&T

AT&T
Communications

AT&T
Technologies

AT&T
International

AT&T
Bell Labs
- Research
- Development

AT&T
Consumer
Products
- Equipment
- Manufacturing

ATTIS: AT&T
Information Services
- Equipment Marketing
- Telephone Rentals

Seven Independent Regional
Companies—ROCs—Formed
from 22 Bell Operating Companies

ROC ROC ROC ROC ROC ROC ROC

Bell
Communications
Research
Organization

- Local Service
- Intrastate Toll Service *within* Exchanges (LATA)
- Licenses on Western Electric Patents
- Yellow Pages
- Bell Name and Logo

    Optional:
- Telephone Rental and/or Sales
- Nontelephone Diversifications

THE REVISED AGREEMENT

On August 11, 1982, Judge Greene issued a 178-page opinion on the original agreement, characterizing it as "plainly in the public interest," but asking modification in ten areas.

The changes he asked for included:

- That the BOCs should continue to have control over the Yellow Pages.

- That the BOCs should be permitted to sell Customer Premises Equipment (telephones and switches, etc.) though prohibited from manufacturing it.

- That provision should be made for further public comment as the plan of implementation was developed, and that he should have adequate opportunity to review public input.

The Justice Department and AT&T accepted all the changes the judge requested, except for permitting the BOCs to sell CPE, which the Justice Department objected to. However, Judge Greene insisted that the BOCs have this right, and the Justice Department conceded the point.

On August 24, 1982, Judge Greene approved the agreement as modified. It then became known in the industry and in the courts as the Modified Final Judgement (MFJ); that is, as a modification of the Final Judgement in the 1956 Consent Decree. (See Figure 3.1.)

4

The Plan of Reorganization

RESTRUCTURING U.S. TELECOMMUNICATIONS SERVICE

Because of AT&T's massive dominance of the nation's telecommunications industry—it had captured 80% of the market in long-distance and more than 90% of the market in local telephone service—a reorganization of AT&T is, in effect, a reorganization of the nation's telecommunications system as a whole. Certainly, it is the farthest-reaching change since the industry's inception.

Although the MFJ contemplated a single Plan of Reorganization to be submitted by AT&T and the Justice Department within six months of the court approval of the MFJ, AT&T adopted a different approach, one dictated by the unprecedented scope of the task ahead. It began immediately to develop discrete elements of the plan, to release them publicly and to submit them to the judge in stages.

There were four different stages in the development and approval of what became the final Plan of Reorganization. First, AT&T, with the help and advice of the Justice Department, determined the number of new BOCs to create. Second, they developed new geographic boundaries within each state defining what would be local service, and therefore the responsibility of the BOCs, and what would be long-distance, and therefore the responsibility of the long-distance companies, such as AT&T and MCI. Third, they drew up the plan for dividing assets between AT&T and the BOCs. Finally, the judge held a separate proceeding to decide remaining controversial issues related to the final plan. His final decision, wrapping up court approval of the Plan of Reorganization, was issued on July 23, 1983, and two weeks

31

later, AT&T held a press conference announcing that it would not appeal this decision.

The Plan of Reorganization was a blueprint for how the nation's phone system was to be restructured. The plan addressed everything from distribution of stock to shareholders, to cancellation of contracts, to transferring employees and pension plans. But from the viewpoint of the regulatory agencies and public interest groups concerned with safeguarding universal service and seeing a more competitive environment, three sections of the plan were the most critical:

1. The ROCs: the number and composition of the Regional Operating Companies (ROCs), new holding companies that would be formed by grouping the BOCs.

2. LATAs: the formation of new geographic areas (Local Access and Transport Areas [LATAs]), which would distinguish local service areas from the long-distance market. The size and shape of these areas would determine the size of the long-distance market as well as which equipment and capital would go to AT&T and which would go to the BOCs.

3. Equal Access: what steps would be taken, and how quickly, to offer all other long-distance companies (the OCCs) the same type, quality and price of access into and out of the BOCs' local exchanges, so that all long-distance companies would be on the same footing as AT&T Long Lines (re-named AT&T Communication Company [ATTCOM] after divestiture) in dealings with the BOCs.

The Regional Operating Companies (ROCs)

Under the plan, the 22 BOCs were reorganized into seven Regional Operating Companies, the fewest number allowed by the MFJ. The ROCs are primarily holding companies whose main business is local telephone service, although they may also engage in unregulated businesses not related to the telephone industry. Each ROC started off with about the same amount of assets—roughly $17 billion (though the territories each encompasses range from two states to fourteen) and roughly the same amount of debts.

The BOCs, which compose the ROCs, have remained largely intact as the familiar Bell operating companies with their pre-divestiture names, such as Pacific Telephone, Illinois Bell, Southern Bell, etc. Table 4.1 lists their contacts in Washington.

The original plan proposed that the Bell name and logo continue to be used jointly by both AT&T and its divested companies, but Judge Greene objected. He ruled that only the divested companies should have ownership of the name and logo, except that Bell Labs and AT&T's international operations would still have the right to them. Accordingly, when the plan was first presented, the ROCs were designated only by regional names (Northeastern Holding Co., Great Lakes Holding Co., etc.) Subsequently, the chief executives assigned to head each ROC by AT&T Chairman Charles Brown chose official names for their respective companies, as given in Table 4.2. Table 4.3 lists the executives of each company and Table 4.4 compares the ROCs as they were on the date of divestiture.

Table 4.1: BOC Region Contacts in Washington, DC

Ameritech (American Information Technology)
John Connarn
Vice President—Federal Relations
(202) 955-3050

1120 20th St., NW
Suite 1000
Washington, DC 20036

Bell Atlantic
Carl Schaubel
Vice President—Federal Relations
(202) 392-6985

1710 Rhode Island Ave., NW
Suite 350
Washington, DC 20006

Bell South
John Brooks
Vice President—Federal Relations
(202) 293-8470

1819 L St., NW
Suite 1000
Washington, DC 20006

Clyde V. Manning
Director—Legislative Matters
(202) 293-8466

NYNEX
Ivan Seidenberg
Vice President—Federal Relations
(202) 955-1150

1825 I St., NW
Room 400
Washington, DC 20006

John Messenger
Washington Counsel
(202) 955-1150

Barbara Morris
Director—Government Relations
(202) 955-1150

Table 4.1: BOC Region Contacts in Washington, DC (Continued)

Ron Sirch
Director—Federal Regulatory Matters
(202) 955-1150

PAC-TEL (Pacific Telesis Group)   444 North Capitol St., NW
Harold Boel   Suite 718
Vice President—Federal Relations   Washington, DC 20001
(202) 383-6408

Colleen Crosland
Director—Federal Relations
(202) 383-6413

Bryant Kidney
Director—Federal Relations
(202) 383-6411

Southwestern Bell Corporation   1667 K St., NW
Robert Dickemper   Suite 200
Vice President—Federal Relations   Washington, DC 20006
(202) 293-8555

Gray Kerrick
Division Staff Manager—Media Relations
(202) 293-8553

U.S. West   1819 L St., NW
Laird Walker   Suite 900
Vice President—Federal Relations   Washington, DC 20036
(202) 293-0558

Wayne Allcott
Executive Director—Legislative Affairs
(202) 224-9778

James A. Smith
Executive Director and
  Attorney—Legislative Affairs
(202) 293-0557

Local Access and Transport Areas

In order for the divestiture to work, it was necessary to devise a way to define local service, to which the BOCs would be restricted, and to distin-

Table 4.2: Division of BOCs Among ROCs

ROC	BOC Included
NYNEX	New England Telephone and Telegraph
	New York Telephone
Bell Atlantic	Bell Telephone of Pennsylvania
	New Jersey Bell Telephone
	Chesapeake & Potomac Telephone
	C&P of Maryland
	C&P of Virginia
	C&P of West Virginia
Bell South	South Central Bell Telephone
	Southern Bell Telephone and Telegraph
Southwestern Bell	The Southwestern Bell Telephone Co.
Ameritech	Illinois Bell Telephone
	Indiana Bell Telephone
	Ohio Bell Telephone
	Michigan Bell Telephone
	Wisconsin Telephone
U.S. West	Northwestern Bell Telephone
	Mountain Bell Telephone
	Pacific Northwest Bell Telephone
Pacific Telesis	The Pacific Telephone & Telegraph Co.
	Nevada Bell

guish it from long-distance service, which AT&T and the other long-distance companies would provide.

This was a critical decision. It defined the areas within which the BOCs could operate. Equally important for AT&T, it determined which plant, equipment and capital stayed with the new AT&T divested companies and which would go to the BOCs. In short, those assets and debits primarily associated with local service were given to the BOCs, and those associated with long-distance service were kept by AT&T.

The task called for a definition of local and long-distance as they would be used after the divestiture. The procedure accepted by the court was to distinguish the two services by carving out new geographic areas within the regions of the divested companies. BOCs would be limited to offering local exchange services *within* those regions. Services *between* those regions would be forbidden to the BOCs and open to AT&T and the OCCs; such service would qualify as long-distance.

Table 4.3: Regional Executives of the Seven ROCs

Designated Chief Executive Officers	Regional Company Entities	Headquarter Addresses and Telephone Numbers
Delbert C. Staley Chairman—NYNEX	NYNEX	1095 Ave. of the Americas 40th Floor New York, NY 10036 (212) 395-2324
	New England Telephone and Telegraph	
William C. Fergusen President—New York Telephone Co.	New York Telephone Co.	
Thomas E. Bolger Chairman—Bell Atlantic	BELL ATLANTIC	5 Penn Center Philadelphia, PA 19103 (215) 963-6300
	Bell Telephone Co. of Pennsylvania	
	Diamond States Telephone Co.	
	Chesapeake and Potomac Cos.	
	New Jersey Bell Telephone Co.	
C.F. Bailey President—South Central Bell Telephone Co.	BELL SOUTH	4507 Southern Bell Center 675 W Peachtree St., NE Atlanta, GA 30375 (404) 529-8611
	South Central Bell Telephone Co.	
B. Franklin Skinner President—Southern Bell Telephone and Telegraph	Southern Bell Telephone and Telegraph	

Table 4.3: Regional Executives of the Seven ROCs (Continued)

	AMERITECH	225 W. Randolph Chicago, IL 60606 (312) 750-5000

Ormand Wade President—Illinois Bell Telephone Co.	**AMERITECH**	225 W. Randolph Chicago, IL 60606 (312) 750-5000
	Illinois Bell Telephone Co.	
	Indiana Bell Telephone Co.	
	Michigan Bell Telephone Co.	
	Ohio Bell Telephone Co.	
	Wisconsin Bell Telephone Co.	
Zane E. Barnes Chairman—Southwestern Bell Telephone Co.	**SOUTHWESTERN BELL TELEPHONE CO.**	1010 Pine St. St. Louis, MO 63101 (314) 247-5400
Jack A. MacAllister President—U.S. WEST	**U.S. WEST**	5700 S. Quebec St. Englewood, CO 80111 (303) 793-6300
	Mountain Bell Telephone Co.	
	Northwestern Bell Telephone	
	Pacific Northwest Bell	
T.J. Saenger President—Pacific Telesis Group, Nevada Bell	**PACIFIC TELESIS GROUP**	140 New Montgomery St. Room 1824 San Francisco, CA 94105 (415) 542-7660
	Nevada Bell	

Table 4.4: Comparison of the Seven ROCs*

	Bell South	NYNEX	Bell Atlantic	Ameritech	Pacific Telesis	Southwestern Bell	U.S. West
Assets	$23,207.2	$18,795.8	$18,197.2	$18,161.2	$17,810.5	$17,491.2	$16,901.3
Revenues	$10,304.2	$ 9,611.6	$ 8,384.4	$ 8,721.9	$ 7,850.1	$ 7,707.0	$ 7,388.7
Net Income	$ 1,232.7	$ 834.9	$ 887.7	$ 849.4	$ 516.6	$ 796.1	$ 762.0
Long-Term Debt	$ 5,890.1	$ 5,188.6	$ 4,759.2	$ 4,942.4	$ 6,559.8	$ 4,675.1	$ 4,416.4
Employees	131,513	120,770	104,825	103,734	106,243	98,783	97,384
Telephones Installed	23,060,313	17,405,016	23,246,096	23,571,025	15,071,681	16,902,639	16,722,270

*As of December 31, 1982. Dollars listed are in millions.

These geographic areas are called Local Access and Transportation Areas—LATAs for short. A LATA is defined as the new exchange area of the post-divestiture world. An exchange area in the LATA sense is different from—usually larger than—the local rate areas or exchange areas defined in state tariffs (primarily for the purpose of designating which intrastate calls are toll calls—those between exchange areas—and which are not). In the new sense, a LATA or exchange area is a regional calling area that can encompass one or more contiguous exchange areas in the old sense and transcends, according to the MFJ, municipal boundaries but generally not state boundaries. It is not the same as an area code, which is merely used for switching and routing calls to distant locations.

As a result of this new definition of exchange, the BOCs were dubbed intraexchange carriers and the OCCs and AT&T, interexchange carriers.

With divestiture, a new trend has developed to better describe this LATA concept—market service areas (MSAs). The service areas concept is viewed more accurately to reflect the function of the new geographic boundaries.

The MFJ gave responsibility to AT&T, working with the Justice Department, to develop the boundaries of the exchange areas for its separated BOCs. The court, however, set guidelines that each LATA (MSA) encompass areas that roughly correspond to Standard Metropolitan Statistical Areas (SMSAs; see below), although it said consideration should also be given to common social and economic characteristics of an area. The MFJ also required that the court approve any LATA with more than one SMSA, or that crossed any state line.

An SMSA is a geographic area defined by the U.S. Office of Management and Budget for the gathering and reporting of federal statistics. In general, it means a large population center along with the communities around it that have a high degree of economic and social integration with that center. There are currently 323 SMSAs in the U.S., and about 75% of the nation's population lives inside a designated SMSA. For example, the Los Angeles–Long Beach SMSA has 7.4 million people; the Boston SMSA has 2.7 million.

With Judge Greene's approval of the Plan of Reorganization, 161 LATAs have been established (as shown in Figure 4.1). Bell South has 37, the most; and Pacific Telesis has 10, the least. Several LATAs correspond to an entire state, such as those for Idaho, Maine, New Mexico and the District of Columbia. But in states where population is denser over a large area, there are several LATAs. New York State has five and Florida has seven.

Prior to divestiture, the BOCs (and independent telephone companies)—not AT&T Long Lines—had the exclusive market for all calls within a state, including all in-state long-distance calls. Now, in-state long-distance that goes from one LATA to another will be the exclusive market of the long-

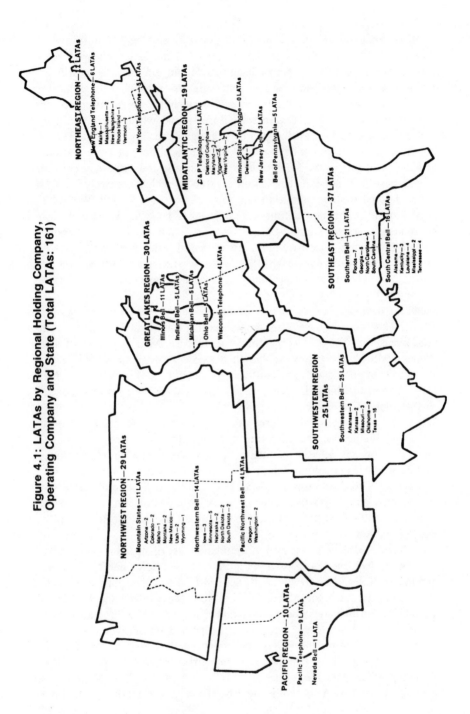

Figure 4.1: LATAs by Regional Holding Company, Operating Company and State (Total LATAs: 161)

distance companies. For example, New York Telephone will no longer be allowed to carry calls between New York City and Buffalo, cities 400 miles apart within the state, because New York City and Buffalo will be in different LATAs. BOCs will still have some toll-call business for calls between distant parts of the same LATAs. This is particularly so in LATAs that cover an entire state (e.g., Wyoming, Nevada, New Mexico). See Table 4.5 for a listing of call categories and Figures 4.2a and 4.2b for the paths by which calls are routed.

The loss of in-state long-distance revenues is being cited by a number of BOCs as reasons they require increases in local rates. In theory, however, the loss of revenues is accompanied by a corresponding loss of responsibility, and therefore, costs. But some operating companies, especially those in large states that collect a lot of long-distance intrastate revenues, such as Texas, claim that in-state long-distance was priced above cost to subsidize local service. Thus the loss of the revenue, they say, will exceed the cost savings by the loss of responsibility to provide the service, and must be replaced by higher local rates.

State PUCs retain jurisdiction over all calls within their state, including calls between LATAs in their state. The PUCs also have the right, if they wish, to allow the interexchange carriers (also called inter-LATA carriers) like AT&T, MCI, ITT, etc. to carry calls within LATAs in their states, though the BOCs are expected to object to this.

The independent telephone companies are not directly affected by the creation of LATAs, nor are they required to establish such areas within their territories. They need not change any of their exchange boundaries. However, calls between independent territories and other independents or LATAs will go to the interexchange carriers. Within a state, the independent company's territory will serve the same function as a LATA.

Equal Access

After divestiture, AT&T's relationship with the divested Bell System companies changed from that of owner to customer. That is, AT&T Communications, AT&T's interexchange (long-distance) division, now has to buy interconnection facilities from the BOCs just as the OCCs have done to connect their long-distance networks with the local exchange networks.

Historically, AT&T Long Lines enjoyed a premium interconnection. It could be seen from the customer point of view when an area code and number was dialed. The call was automatically routed over AT&T Long Lines facilities. The OCCs, however, have not had such direct access to the cus-

Figure 4.2a: A State With Only One LATA

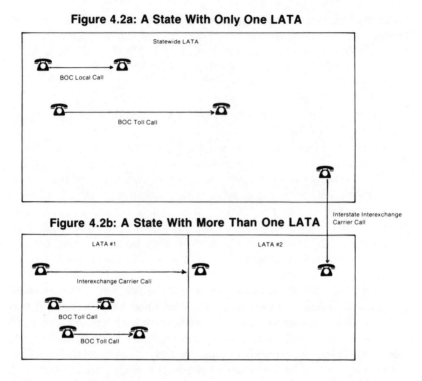

Figure 4.2b: A State With More Than One LATA

tomer or to the local exchange. In order to connect to an OCC, the customer must, in most cases, use a touch-tone–type phone and dial up to 12 extra numbers, on top of the 10 associated with the area code and number. And the facilities used to connect the OCC calls to the local exchange are inferior to those that are available to AT&T, so OCC customers may experience static or weak connections on their long-distance calls.

The difference in local interconnection between AT&T and the OCCs did not change immediately on January 1, 1984. Achieving equal access is going to require a major construction program. The MFJ calls for all interexchange carriers to be treated by the BOCs on a "tariffed basis that is equal in type, quality and prices." This means that the BOCs must install facilities to offer all interexchange carriers the same quality of access—equal access—as that given AT&T. And until that happens, AT&T will continue to pay a premium charge for its premium access.

For interexchange carriers, such as MCI, GTE-Sprint and AT&T, to offer long-distance service to any area, they must establish what is known as a Point of Presence (POP) within the regional calling area to be served (LATA). Once a POP is established, the local company (BOC) and the

Table 4.5: Categories of Local and Long-Distance Calls After Divestiture

Description	Category	Regulated By	Common Name	Carried By
Calls within community or municipality	*Intra*-LATA Intrastate	State PUC	Local	BOC
Calls to distant point within same exchange	*Intra*-LATA Intrastate	State PUC	Toll	BOC
Calls to another exchange within state	*Inter*-LATA Intrastate	State PUC	Long-Distance	Long-Distance Companies
Calls to another exchange in another state	*Inter*-LATA Interstate	FCC	Long-Distance*	Long-Distance Companies

LATA = Exchange = (approximately) SMSA

Intra-LATA = Intraexchange = Carried exclusively by BOC

Inter-LATA = Interexchange = Carried exclusively by AT&T, MCI, GTE-Sprint, etc. (Long-distance carriers)

*Not every call to another exchange in another state is a long-distance or toll call; for example, a call from Washington, D.C., to Arlington, VA, a suburb of Washington, is an inter-LATA, interstate call, but it is still a local call for which there is no long-distance charge, even though it is carried by one of the long-distance companies (interexchange carriers).

long-distance company arrange to transfer the calls from the POP through trunk lines to a local switching facility, often called wire centers. The type of equipment used to connect the trunk from the POP to the wire center determines the type of access. Once OCCs have equal access, consumers will be given the opportunity to choose the long-distance company that will carry their calls whenever they dial the area code and number.

A major issue that developed during the divestiture proceeding was whether the cost of equal access should be borne by the BOCs or the interexchange carriers. The cost of the BOC construction program to establish new equal access to measure the amount of long-distance calling that comes in from each OCC is in the billions of dollars. In his final decision on the divestiture, Judge Greene held that the interexchange companies must pay the total cost of equal access, not the BOCs.

Since it will take time for BOCs to make the necessary changes to install POP facilities in their switching facilities, the MFJ set a phase-in schedule, as follows:

- September 1, 1984: Local companies must begin to offer equal access.

- September 1, 1985: One-third of all local companies' equal-access lines must be in service.

- September 1, 1986: All local exchanges must have completed installation of equal-access facilities where they have been requested by long-distance companies, except where modification of facilities would be uneconomical or where exchanges serve fewer than 10,000 lines.

The National Exchange Carrier Association Tariffs

Since, under the terms of the divestiture, AT&T has become a customer rather than an owner of the local exchanges, AT&T has begun paying for local access services just as the other long-distance carriers (OCCs) have been doing.

To provide for this, the FCC ordered the BOCs and the independent telephone companies to form a new organization, to be called the National Exchange Carrier Association (NECA). This organization is responsible for filing and collecting interstate access-charge tariffs on AT&T and all the other long-distance carriers. The NECA tariffs replace the DR procedure within the Bell System before divestiture, whereby, in addition to revenue-sharing between the BOCs and Long Lines, the BOCs were reimbursed for their costs in providing access services to Long Lines. The NECA tariffs also replace the ENFIA tariffs.

Under tariffs filed by the BOCs and the independents on September 30, 1983 and eventually approved on May 17, 1984 to become effective on May 15, 1984, the NECA tariffs will consist of:

1. a per-minute (AT&T) or a per-line (OCC) charge for access to BOC switching and trunking facilities that originate and terminate long-distance calls;

2. a per-minute-of-use charge on fixed access facilities (the local loop wires and other facilities connecting customer phones with the central switching office—a cost not related to the amount of customer use); and

3. charges for specific services provided directly to interexchange carriers—primarily AT&T, such as billing and operator-information services.

Under the customer access fee proposed by the FCC the fixed access charge (the second charge described above) would decline over time for all long-distance carriers. It would gradually be replaced by the FCC-mandated access charge to be paid by local customers.

But until the OCCs have access facilities equal to those of AT&T, these companies continue to pay the less costly flat rate charges for trunking and switching and less on fixed access charges. This payment differential for the OCCs follows the precedent set by ENFIA rates before divestiture. Despite such discounted rates, the OCCs vigorously protested because the proposed new rates would have almost doubled what they had been paying prior to divestiture.

5

The Repricing Movement

Perhaps the greatest public concern about divestiture has been connected with warnings from state regulators and public interest groups that local telephone rates would double and triple within a few years. The FCC Consumer Access Line Charges (CALCs) proposed for all local customers (discussed later in this chapter) have been hotly debated; legislation in Congress to block them passed the House of Representatives in the fall, but died in the Senate when no action was taken by the end of the Congress in October 1984.

On top of that, nearly every BOC filed requests either prior to divestiture or shortly thereafter for hefty increases in basic residential rates. Southwestern Bell asked for a $1.2 billion increase—an amount that would triple local bills for its Texas customers. Pacific Telephone sought a $1.3 billion increase, which would boost monthly charges from $7 to $18. Michigan Bell requested a $450 million increase and C&P of Maryland asked for $218 million. In all, the BOCs filed rate increase requests totaling more than $9 billion in 30 states.

There is, however, a popular misconception in blaming these rate increases on the divestiture. Rather, these rate increase requests, along with the planned FCC CALC, are part of a separate change in the industry that had been underway long before the divestiture agreement was made and is happening for reasons only partly connected with the restructuring of the industry.

The real phenomenon behind this rate change activity is repricing. It is the pressure to shift the burden of cost recovery directly onto each part of telecommunications service that creates each cost. In its most basic manifestation, it entails higher rates for local service and lower rates for long-distance service.

The main force behind the repricing movement is the entry of competition into a once thoroughly regulated industry. With the emergence of the OCCs, whose prime marketing strategy has been to undercut AT&T rates for long-distance service, AT&T began to argue forcefully with the FCC that it was unfair to require AT&T's long-distance rates to subsidize local service so that the ideal of universal service—high-quality service available at affordable rates to the entire population—could be maintained.

Since the 1930 Supreme Court decision, *Smith v. Illinois* (see Chapter 3), and the passage of the 1934 Communications Act, long-distance prices have been gradually raised in order to contribute more to local service. Local telephone companies claim it now costs an average of $26 a month to cover just the fixed cost associated with the nation's 200 million telephone lines, while in 1983 the typical household paid an average of only $9.16 a month for this service. The rest has to come from other sources of revenues—other local services, such as pay telephones, and from revenues on long-distance provided primarily by the Division of Revenues system and in part from ENFIA tariffs paid by the OCCs (see Chapter 3).

Not everyone agrees that all long-distance payments to local companies are subsidies, that is, giveaways from long-distance companies to the local operating companies. A considerable portion of the DR is said by some to have been reimbursements and profits due the BOCs in return for access services and for BOC investments in facilities for switching calls between the local network and the long-distance networks.

Nevertheless, the FCC has been moving toward the point-of-view that competition in telecommunications will benefit the public, and that in the world of competition every service or product should be priced according to its cost if a business that offers it is to survive. AT&T argued that by being required to price its services artificially high (long-distance service) and artificially low (local service), it was unable to compete fairly with those companies that were selling lower-cost long-distance service.

As far back as 1978, four years before the divestiture agreement, the FCC began an inquiry into this long-distance subsidy issue, focusing on the question of revising the FCC formula for sharing long-distance revenues between local and long-distance operations.

THE LOCAL LOOP AND THE ACCESS FEE

The FCC inquiry led to an examination of the cost of the local loop—the telephone company's facilities that connect the local telephone customers to their exchange's central office, and what fee—access fee—should be paid by the long-distance operation toward the cost of maintaining that loop. The local loop is necessary for making both local calls and long-distance calls. In the short term, its cost is generally fixed—remaining the same whether the customer uses the phone or not. The customer encounters the local loop through the dial tone that sounds when the phone receiver is lifted off the hook. It signals that the customer is connected to the switching equipment in the local BOC office and can therefore make and receive calls on the local, national and international networks.

Long-distance revenues (both interstate and intrastate) have provided approximately half of the estimated $25 billion current costs of providing the local loop in the Bell System. AT&T argued, and the FCC agreed, that this was an unfairly high share for the long-distance customer, who was being charged artificially high long-distance rates to cover this disproportionate share of access costs.

On December 22, 1982, the FCC adopted an access-charge plan to shift most of the fixed costs of the local loop away from the long-distance user and onto the local customer. The plan, as proposed, was to become effective concurrent with the AT&T divestiture on January 1, 1984.[1]

The FCC order ("In the Matter of MTS and WATS Market Structure, CC Docket No. 78–72, Phase I, Third Report and Order") imposes a new fee, the Customer Access Lines Charge (CALC) on all local ratepayers, ostensibly to pay the cost of long-distance access through the local loop, though the fee was to apply whether or not the customer used long-distance service. The CALC would be added to the basic monthly charge for local service, which represented to the FCC a transfer of cost from the long-distance user to the true cost causer, namely, the local customer whose phone is tied into the long-distance system through the local loop.

The FCC plan would be phased in over a period of six years beginning in 1984, increasing gradually, while the charges to the long-distance companies for the local loop would decrease until most of the cost was shifted to the local customer, according to the following schedule in Table 5.1.*

---

1. The plan created a storm of protest from consumer groups as well as legislation in the House and Senate opposing it. In reaction to this, the FCC twice delayed implementing the plan. The legislation and the nature of the FCC delays is presented in detail later in this chapter under the discussion on Congressional legislation.

---

*As this book went to press, a panel of Federal and state regulators, the Federal-State Communications Joint Board, recommended that the monthly residential access fee be cut in half to $1 a month, starting in June 1985. In 1986, however, it will rise to $2 a month. The FCC will vote on this recommendation in December 1984.

Table 5.1: Maximum Access Fee, Per Month, Per Line

	Residential Ratepayer	Business Ratepayer
1984:	$2	$6
1985:	$3	$6
1986:	$4	$6

Between 1986 and 1990, the CALC would continue to increase, but the FCC did not specify the precise amounts. Instead, it established a formula that would be used to decide how much of the remaining fixed local loop costs needed to be transfered from long-distance users to the local customer. It is generally believed that for most areas the CALC cost for the residential customers will be $10.50 per line, per month. But the charge may be less, depending on the jurisdiction and the actual cost of the local loop.

The CALC is set by BOCs in tariffs filed with the FCC. Initial filings occured on October 3, 1983. All states proposed to impose the authorized $2.00 CALC for residential customers, but many proposed a CALC below the authorized $6.00 for businesses.

Since the FCC regulates only interstate rates and service, its decision could only apply to the transfer of costs from interstate long-distance markets to the local loop customer. A number of BOCs took their lead from the FCC and filed requests at state PUCs to impose an intrastate CALC similar to that adopted by the FCC.

Because of divestiture and its resulting change in jurisdiction over which company provides in-state long-distance service (see Chapter 5), each state had to come up with its own plan for charging in-state long-distance companies for access to the local exchange.

If states follow the model established by the FCC access-charge decision, then the fixed costs of the local loop now paid for as part of the in-state long-distance charges, will be transformed into a CALC to be added to the local customer's bill on top of local service charges and on top of the FCC CALC.

Initially, some states and local companies have chosen not to follow the FCC access-charge scheme and, instead, intend to continue to recover some of the local loop fixed costs from the in-state long-distance users. Indeed, as of August 1984, of those states that had considered whether to impose a consumer access charge, none had done so. Although Illinois and Washington State adopted the charge, both later suspended it. New Mexico adopted the charge but only for areas associated with non-New Mexico LATAs.

The following states have considered the issue and have decided not to impose an intrastate consumer access line charge:[1]

Alabama*	Nebraska
Arizona*	Nevada
California*	New Jersey*
Colorado	New York*
Delaware*	North Carolina
Florida	North Dakota
Georgia*	Ohio
Idaho	Oklahoma
Illinois	Oregon*
Iowa	Pennsylvania
Kansas*	South Carolina
Louisiana	Tennessee
Maryland	Texas
Massachusetts	Virginia
Michigan*	Washington
Minnesota*	West Virginia*
Mississippi*	Wisconsin
Missouri*	Wyoming
Montana*	

THE BYPASS ISSUE

The FCC's decision to shift the cost of the local loop to the local customer was prompted not only by its desire to allocate costs to what it considered to be the real cost causer. The agency was also motivated by concern about how artificially high long-distance costs were creating a new phenomenon called bypass.

Bypass occurs when telephone company customers decide they can provide their own telephone service more cheaply than through a regulated telephone company whose rates are set by governmental agencies. Bypass can occur either locally or in the long-distance market, and typically involves

---

1. States indicated with an asterisk (*) have issued only interim orders and may reconsider their decision at a later date. States not listed have not considered the question, usually because the BOC has not requested an in-state CALC.

giant corporations or government agencies that spend $30 million to $100 million or more each year in telephone costs. To bypass, a company buys or leases its own lines or facilities to complete its transmission without going through the BOC exchange. Figures 5.1 and 5.2 show a typical long-distance configuration, without and with bypass.

The FCC's primary concern is bypass by long-distance users. Under the old scheme, long-distance users were paying a substantial portion of the fixed local loop costs. Payment took the form of higher per-minute rates paid to AT&T, which then paid the BOCs for the local loop costs. The FCC estimated that about 13 cents per minute of each long-distance call represented money paid to the BOCs for the local fixed costs. That meant heavy telephone users were paying that 13 cents over and over again, while the light users were not contributing very much toward the local loop costs.

With the development of new communications technologies, the threat of bypass has become a reality in more and more cases, according to the FCC. A company could now buy or lease its own long-distance system, including facilities to bypass the local exchange, by installing microwave or satellite transmission antennas on roofs of their plants and offices. The important thing would be to avoid the 13 cents per minute charge on each call, which would be collected only if a call went through the BOC's facilities. Thus, a

Figure 5.1: Local Loop Configuration—No Bypass

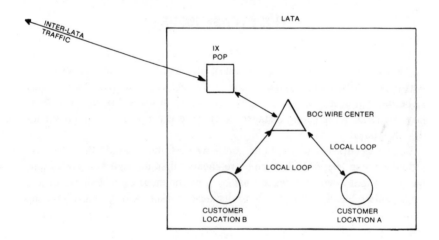

KEY: IX POP = INTEREXCHANGE CARRIER'S POINT-OF-PRESENCE
     LATA   = LOCAL ACCESS TRANSPORT AREA

Figure 5.2: Bypass Configuration

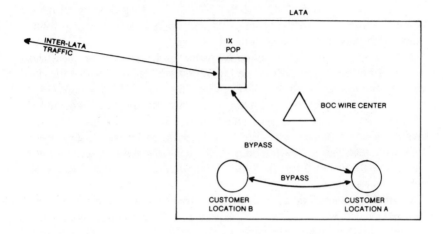

KEY: IX POP = INTEREXCHANGE CARRIER'S POINT-OF-PRESENCE
       LATA   = LOCAL ACCESS TRANSPORT AREA

company could also bypass the BOC switch by hooking up directly to a long-distance carrier, such as AT&T.

In fact, the FCC's concerns about bypass were prompted in large part by the fact that after divestiture, AT&T itself would have no incentive to stay with the local BOC. In the past, AT&T owned the investment in the local company, and therefore it made sense for AT&T to run its long-distance calls through the local company. After divestiture, though, AT&T is just like any other long-distance company with no financial interest in the BOC. Thus, AT&T, in looking after its long-distance customers, would be inclined to find a way to reduce the local loop portion of its costs through bypass.

The FCC was concerned that a large volume of local service revenues could be lost by the local BOC through extensive bypass. If this happened on a large scale, the financial viability of the local BOC—and therefore the quality of service available to the local community—could be threatened. It would also mean high rates for local customers—those who don't have the choice to bypass and must stay on the system—to offset the lost revenue from bypass.

Bypass may seem relatively insignificant if one envisions only a few very big companies choosing to set up their own long-distance systems. But among business users of long-distance service, the Bell System's revenues are usually concentrated among a very limited number of large business customers. (See Figure 5.3.) Typically, 30% of all long-distance revenues come from only 1% of the business customers. And 50% of the revenues come from only 5% of the customer base.

Indeed, the long-distance usage by both residential and business customers is highly concentrated. (See Figure 5.4.) AT&T claims that unless it can reduce its costs and have greater pricing flexibility, that its new competitors will unfairly skim the cream of its markets. In mid-1984, AT&T claimed that 73% of residential telephone users spent less than $10 each month on long-distance calls. Eighty-six percent of business users reportedly spent less than $50 each month. And 0.1% of business users reportedly accounted for about 20% of AT&T's long-distance revenues, which are reported in Table 5.2.

By making long-distance rates lower through shifting local loop fixed costs to local subscribers, the FCC expects that there will be less economic incentive for large organizations to bypass. Many BOCs, for the same reasons, are urging state PUCs to follow the FCC's lead and impose a similar CALC to shift the fixed cost of the local loop from intrastate long-distance callers.

Table 5.2: Residential and Business Long-Distance Usage

RESIDENTIAL USERS	
Less than $10 a month in long-distance service	73%
$10 to $25 a month in long-distance service	17%
More than $25 a month in long-distance service	10%
BUSINESS USERS	
Less than $50 a month in long-distance service	86%
More than $50 a month in long-distance service	14%

Source: AT&T

CONGRESSIONAL LEGISLATION ON THE FCC ACCESS FEE

Although the FCC access-fee scheme was announced in December 1982, it received little public attention until July 1983, when the Commission issued what it intended to be a final ruling on what had been several petitions for reconsideration of the December action. The July decision triggered widespread protests.

Figure 5.3: Telephone Company Business Revenues Are Usually Concentrated Among a Limited Number of Large Business Customers

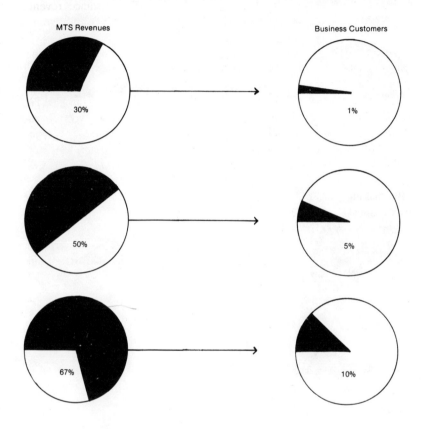

Source: Touche Ross and Co.

Consumers, already faced with local rate increase proposals of $9 billion, learned for the first time that there would be a new FCC charge on their bills. The protests by members of the House that the new charges would take effect at the beginning of an election year revived congressional concern about telecommunications policy in the summer of 1983, even though only a year before, House Telecommunications Committee Chairman Timothy Wirth (D-CO) and House Energy and Commerce Committee chairman John Dingell (D-MI) had abandoned the latest attempts to push through a telecommunications reform bill.

**Figure 5.4: Telephone Company Revenues
May Also Be Concentrated Geographically**

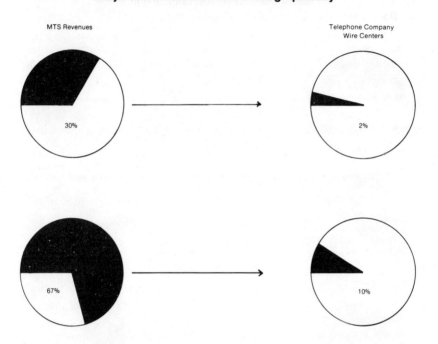

Source: Touche Ross and Co.

The House

Strong opposition from AT&T had led to the death of the earlier House bill (H.R. 5158). But the access fee had become such a hot issue that Wirth quickly put together H.R. 3621 and moved it out of the subcommittee early in October. AT&T strongly opposed the bill and again launched a grass roots lobbying campaign to stop the progress of legislation in the full House Energy and Commerce Committee. AT&T had been successful the last time, but it failed this time, when on October 27, 1983, the Commerce Committee voted to report the bill, as amended, to the full House. The vote was 27 to 15 in favor of the bill, with all 27 yea votes coming from Democratic members of the committee and the 15 nay votes coming from Republican members.

As reported and amended, the bill acquired a new number—H.R. 4102. It was cleared by the Rules Committee for floor action in early November, and floor action was scheduled for the 8th. A vote was taken on November 10, and the bill was passed by a voice vote.

The House bill, if it had become law, would have established an entirely new framework for assessing charges to long-distance carriers and for the redistribution of the revenues collected from those charges. The key provisions of H.R. 4102, as it passed the House, were as follows:

- All flat monthly charges (CALCs) on residential and single-line business subscribers were prohibited.

- A business CALC for second and subsequent business lines was permitted.

- Long-distance companies were required to pay a share of the joint and common fixed local loop costs. They also had to pay a fee toward a Universal Service Fund, created to subsidize rural high-cost areas and BOCs for local lifeline service.

- Bypass would still be legal, but bypassers were going to be required to make payments to the BOC based on three factors: if there was interconnection with the local loop, a fee based on the nature and extent of the interconnection; a fee to the BOC for the use of the BOC's facilities as a back up to their privately owned facilities; and a fee to the Universal Service Fund, just like the ones the long-distance companies were going to pay.

- The Universal Service Fund established detailed formulas for distribution of money to rural areas. Urban areas were permitted to recover 50% of their costs for lifeline service.

- States were required to set up lifeline rates for low-income residential customers meeting federal welfare criteria.

- Reimbursement of costs for public participation in federal FCC rate-making proceedings were provided for.

- Each state was required to set up an agency to represent telephone consumers in state rate proceedings. These would be nongovernmental organizations funded through voluntary contributions. The legislation gave the groups the right to send mailings to telephone customers with the local telephone bill.

- It reversed that part of the FCC decision that increased the cost of access by the OCCs relative to what AT&T had been paying. Previously, the ENFIA charges paid by the OCCs had been roughly 55% less than the amount paid by AT&T Long Lines for access to the local exchange. The FCC access decision reduced the differential to 35%. The legislation would restore the 55% differential until equal access.

- It provided for significant fines against any company that bypassed the local telephone company plan and did not pay the universal service or interconnection charges.

The Senate

Senate Commerce Committee Chairman Robert Packwood (R-OR) also responded to the public pressures generated by the FCC access-fee decision and introduced his own bill—S. 1660. In an unusual move, Sen. Packwood agreed to hold the hearings on his bill jointly with the House Committee on Commerce, which was considering Rep. Wirth's bill. As introduced, S. 1660 and H.R. 3621 (which became H.R. 4102) were similar in their provisions.

But Sen. Packwood did not have the same support for his legislation that Rep. Wirth found in the House. Initial efforts to pass S. 1660 out of committee ran into serious problems. Instead of supporting Packwood's approach, the committee members favored an approach offered by Sen. Lautenberg (D-NJ), which would have merely delayed implementation of the access fee. Following intense negotiations, the Senate Commerce Committee met on October 7, 1983, and acted to report S. 1660 to the floor of the Senate.

The key provisions of the Senate bill:

- Delayed the imposition of residential or one-line business CALCs until January 1, 1986;

- assessed a universal service charge to long-distance carriers and bypassers, which would be made into a Universal Service Fund;

- provided for the distribution of the revenues to the high-cost rural areas, according to a detailed formula;

- provided for distribution of revenues to states offering lifeline services to low-income residential users to reimburse for the cost of lifeline; and

- provided for a $100,000 fine for failure to pay the universal service
  surcharge.

(See Figure 5.5 for a comparison of the FCC plan and the Senate bill.)
S. 1660 was scheduled to be taken up on the Senate floor as the first item
of business when Congress reconvened at the end of January 1984. The passage of H.R. 4102 in November 1983, and a grass roots campaign by consumer groups created a political environment on the issue that made it appear likely that the Senate bill would also pass. However, the Senate later
voted not to consider S. 1660.

FCC RESPONSE TO CONGRESSIONAL PRESSURE: DELAYS IN IMPLEMENTING THE ACCESS FEES

When it became clear in November 1983, with the movement of H.R.
4102 out of committee, that a groundswell of consumer opposition to
access-fee charges was developing, the FCC was put on the defensive.

In December, the FCC announced a delay in implementing the plan,
originally scheduled to go into effect simultaneously with the AT&T divestiture on January 1, 1984. It moved the implementation date back to April 3,
1984, for two reasons.

First, it found the information submitted by the BOCs in support of
the access fees they proposed to charge consumers and long-distance
companies inadequate. The FCC could not approve them to go into effect on
January 1.

Second, the FCC expressed disappointment in the size of the proposed
reduction in AT&T's long-distance rates. It was this reduction in the cost of
long-distance service that the FCC hoped would offset the public and congressional opposition to its plan. Thus, the commission, in delaying the effective date of the access-fee plan, also cited the need to review AT&T's revised rates in greater detail.

In the interim between January 1 and April 3, AT&T continued to pay the
BOCs essentially the same rate as it had before divestiture. The company
protested vehemently but to no avail.

Despite this delay, however, H.R. 4102 went to the floor of the House
and passed. Passage of the Senate version was looming, and with it the

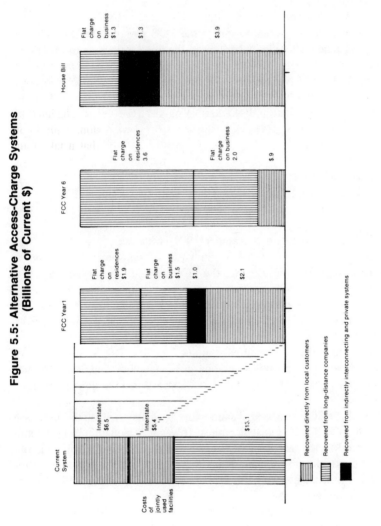

**Figure 5.5: Alternative Access-Charge Systems
(Billions of Current $)**

Source: House Committee on Commerce and Science

likelihood that the FCC would have its authority to impose the access fee either eliminated or severely limited. Indeed, there appeared to be overwhelming support in the Senate for passage of S. 1660 and its delay of access fees until after the 1984 elections.

But supporters of the FCC plan knew that Sen. Packwood was much more sympathetic to the House bill than to the Senate bill, which had been changed in Committee over his objections. They were afraid to pass S. 1660 and have it go to conference with H.R. 4102 with Sen. Packwood in charge of the negotiations. It became clear to AT&T and other supporters of access fees, which now included the Reagan administration, that the only possible way to save the access-fee concept was to convince the FCC to back down from its plan to implement residential access-line charges.

On January 17, 1984, about one week before the Senate was scheduled to reconvene and take up S. 1660, Sen. Robert Dole (R-KS), along with 36 of his Republican colleagues, sent a letter to the FCC asking that it take four specific actions:

1. Prohibit telephone companies from imposing flat-rate end-user charges on residential and single-line business customers during 1984.

2. Let each small telephone company decide for itself whether to impose end-user charges on residential and single-line business customers.

3. Cap the flat-rate end-user charge for all the residential and single-line business customers of larger telephone companies at $4.00 until at least 1990.

4. Substantially lessen the amount of increase in the interconnection charge (the old ENFIA charge) that the OCCs would pay to the BOCs.

On January 19, 1984, only two days after the delivery of the Dole letter, the FCC met and decided to make changes in its access-fee plan. In a press release issued that day, the FCC said it was taking a course of action almost identical to that suggested in the Dole letter. In what it described as a tentative decision to be made final on January 25, the commission announced that:

1. It delayed implementation of the access charge for residential and single-line business customers throughout 1984. Further, it said that it was now the view of the FCC that the residential CALC should be gradually phased in, stretching to 1990 and capped at $4.00.

2. It directed its staff to begin an inquiry on how to provide greater aid to smaller telephone companies.

3. It proposed further study of the impact of its decisions on universal telephone service.

4. It called for additional study of the bypass phenomenon and its impact on local telephone companies.

5. It also reduced the amount that the OCCs were to pay to the BOCs during the transition period to equal access.

The effect of this delay was to defuse the pressure to pass a Senate bill in 1984, since the FCC action accomplished most of what was proposed in S. 1660. On January 26, the day after the FCC's revised plan was final, the Senate voted not to proceed with consideration of S. 1660 by a vote of 44 to 40.

The business CALC (for businesses with more than one line), was not included in the FCC delay and was still scheduled to go into effect on April 3, 1984. However, even in this area the FCC continued to have difficulty in arriving at a workable plan. In March, it again announced a delay in implementation of the business CALC until June 13, 1984.

On May 10, 1984, the commission issued a decision clearing the way for the CALC to go into effect on June 13. Its decision resolved all outstanding issues concerning the business CALC, reduction in AT&T long-distance rates, whether to change the ENFIA formula again, the implementation of a charge for long-distance information use and how much the BOCs could collect from AT&T and other interexchange carriers for billing and similar services. The key features of the May 10 decision were:

1. Multiline business customers (all businesses with more than one line) would begin paying a montly CALC on June 13 of up to $6.00.

2. AT&T long-distance rates would be reduced 6.1% across the board.

3. The amount requested by the BOCs for their services was reduced by 8.5%.

4. The reduced payments for the OCCs adopted in January were left unchanged, despite a petition for "emergency relief" by AT&T challenging that action.

5. A charge of 50 cents per long-distance information call was instituted. An allowance of two free information calls per month was provided for consumers who make at least two long-distance calls over AT&T's system.

Pros and Cons of the FCC Access-Fee Decision

With the residential CALC delayed and congressional action on telecommunications in 1984 virtually dead, the access fee receded as a major political issue. However, as of late 1984 the access-fee plan had not gone away. Indeed, the FCC made it clear in its May 10, 1984 decision that it continues to believe in and support the underlying pricing theory behind consumer access-line charges.

The controversy over access fees will undoubtedly continue when the FCC completes its year-long study around the end of 1984. Rep. John Dingell and Sen. Robert Packwood both have publicly alerted the FCC of their intention to take up the anti–access-fee battle again if need be. Indeed, more than 190 members of the House of Representatives signed a petition in May 1984 asking the FCC to delay the implementation of the business CALCs for a year. Thus, it is clear that the debate over access fees will continue for some time to come.

Proponents of the fee, primarily AT&T and the other long-distance companies, make the following arguments in its defense:

- The laws of economics require the shift to cost-justified pricing if long-distance telecommunications are to move from a monopoly structure to a fully competitive one.

- The competition stimulated by repricing will stimulate the technological innovation needed to maintain U.S. prominence in telecommunications, the key industry of the 1980s.

- The repricing will not substantially increase the overall cost of telephone service for most consumers because the access fee will be offset by lower rates for long-distance and competition in the equipment markets. AT&T's long-distance rates were ordered to be lowered by 6.1% just based upon the business CALC. More substantial reductions are likely upon the full implementation of CALCs. The FCC predicts reductions of up to 30% or 40% of pre–access-fee levels.

- Without the fee shift to consumers, it will not be possible to lower long-distance costs to their true level and thereby discourage large companies from uneconomical bypass. Once a company installs a by-pass system it is lost permanently from the local revenue base, because such systems are so expensive it becomes uneconomical to dismantle them.

Opponents of the fee, mainly consumers and state regulators who have made their views known to members of Congress, argue that:

- The access fee is a threat to universal service. It will increase local rates and force many people, especially the poor and near-poor, to drop off the telephone system because they will no longer be able to afford having a phone. They contend that by 1990 the interstate access fee, combined with the intrastate access fees already being requested by the BOCs so they can lower their intrastate rates, will be close to $20 a month—just for a dial tone, before even using the phone. They cite Department of Commerce statistics—as detailed in Figure 5.6—that project that the 91.5% of American households with basic telephone service in 1980 might drop to 83.7% by 1989 if local charges increase by 100%, as they would when the access fee is fully shifted to the consumer.

- The cost causer concept adopted by the FCC attributing the non-traffic-sensitive cost of the local loop to the local customer is not valid. The local loop is a joint and common cost—attributable to all its uses—local, in-state and interstate calling. Each class of customer, therefore, should contribute revenue to paying those costs. The FCC decision unfairly places the full local loop burden on the local customer—in effect creating a reverse subsidy.

- Bypass is not exclusively a long-distance problem. By transferring costs from long-distance to local markets, the FCC is merely shifting the incentive to bypass to the local exchange. Technology to bypass local loops also exists and is being used. First, bypass occurs by simple reduction of the number of local lines a company has. Second, it occurs by use of microwave and other direct connection facilities. Moreover, the concentration of long-distance use exists in local usage—but worse. One percent of local customers typically account for 50% of the BOC revenue. An FCC CALC, by attributing full local loop costs to each customer line, is creating uneconomical incentives to bypass the local loop.

- The FCC has sought to deal with the long-distance bypass problem in the wrong way: by reducing costs so that companies won't bypass, instead of making it less economical to bypass, as Congress proposes, by imposing a fee on bypassers.

- The true beneficiaries of the long-distance and local phone systems are those who use them the most. These are the largest 1% to 5% of the telephone customers accounting for the 30% to 50% of the long-distance revenues. They are the true cost causers, because their demand on the local and long-distance systems is the greatest. And in any case, these relatively few users are more able to absorb the costs of the local loop than the residential and small business or light user of the phone system.

**Figure 5.6: Estimated Percentage of Households
with Basic Telephone Service**

Demographic characteristics	Price Increase			
	Base	50%	100%	200%
All:	**91.52**	**88.15**	**83.69**	**70.92**
Young	85.39	80.12	73.54	56.92
Black	86.37	81.38	75.08	58.89
Rural	88.84	84.59	79.10	64.28
Moderately Poor:	**83.81**	**78.12**	**71.11**	**53.93**
Young	72.18	64.14	55.22	36.97
Black	75.25	67.71	59.12	40.74
Rural	79.26	72.48	64.50	46.34
Very Poor:	**79.28**	**72.52**	**64.53**	**46.38**
Young	64.99	56.14	46.88	29.56
Black	69.21	60.78	51.66	33.69
Rural	73.85	66.07	57.31	38.96

Source: Household demographic and economic data: U.S. Dept. of Commerce, Bureau of the Census, *Money Income of Households in the United States: 1979* (Washington, DC: U.S. Government Printing Office). U.S. Dept. of Commerce, Bureau of the Census, *Household and Family Characteristics: March 1980* (Washington, DC: U.S. Government Printing Office).

Telephone rate information: American Telephone and Telegraph Co., Market and Service Plans Department, Research Section, Market Research Information Systems (MRIS).

From: Memorandum Order and Opinion, in re MTS and WATS Market Structure FCC Docket No. 78–72, December 22, 1982.

LOCAL MEASURED SERVICE AND UNBUNDLING

In addition to the shift in costs from long-distance to local service, the repricing movement also extends to a new look at how the components of local service itself are priced. Here the push is the same as in pricing for long-distance: the idea that each facet of service should pay its own way. This is sometimes called unbundling of costs.

A big issue is the continued availability of unlimited flat-rate service, whereby states require the local companies to make local service available at a single flat fee, regardless of how much or how little each customer uses the service. The Bell companies object to this, claiming that rising costs and marked disparities in usage require that calls should be charged for on a per-call basis. Twenty percent of their residential customers, on the average, make 45% of all residential calls, and 20% make only 5% of all the residential calls. Bell wants Local Measured Service (LMS). Under this method, every call is charged for by: 1) duration, 2) time of day, 3) distance and 4) frequency (a unit charge for each call). That's basically the same as charges on long-distance calls.

The Bell companies claim LMS is a fairer method, charging people only for what they use. They point out that for many consumers, LMS would mean lower monthly bills for local service. And it has been in effect for several years in a few communities, such as New York City, where local calls are charged for by message units. For a detailed listing of regions where LMS is available, see Table 5.3.

However, critics claim that LMS is unfair. They argue that it is just another means of increasing company revenues by making the billing system too complex for the average consumer to understand or control. They also claim that the cost justifications offered by the company don't wash; that it actually costs more to measure service, and as a result it will force rates up. Finally, they dispute the BOC's claims that LMS is cost-justified. They say that it is not possible to pinpoint costs of the factors the company wants to measure.

Implementation of LMS historically has been a priority for the Bell System. At the same time, it has been the lightning rod for most consumer involvement in state rate proceedings. More recently, operating companies have proposed a new version of measured service. Called Optional Measured Service (OMS), the new rate is proposed by the BOCs as a lower-cost option for consumers who can't afford the higher rates being proposed because of repricing.

Fairness is not the only reason Bell is arguing for LMS. Another motive is the rise in the number of computer users who transmit data by phone, of-

Table 5.3: Local Measured Service Scorecard

Listed are states that have any rate plan that involves charging for local calls by the minute or by distance. Some states listed have LMS only in certain counties or in areas served by electronic switching equipment. Others have LMS only on an experimental basis. States that have an experiment are noted.

State	Status	Company	Effective Date
Alabama	No	South Central Bell	
Arizona	Optional	Mountain Bell	January 1, 1983
Arkansas	Optional	Southwest Bell	July 1980
California	Optional	Pacific Bell	January 1977
Colorado	Optional	Mountain Bell	September 1, 1983
Connecticut	Optional	Southern New England Tel.	December 1982
Delaware	Optional	Diamond State Tel.	August 19, 1980
District of Columbia	No	C&P Telephone	
Florida	Experimental	Southern Bell	December 31, 1978
Georgia	Experimental	Southern Bell	May 15, 1980
Idaho	Optional	Mountain Bell	August 23, 1983
Illinois	Optional	GTE Telephone Cos.	March 1, 1983
Indiana	No	Indiana Bell	
	No	General Telephone	
Iowa	Experimental	Northwest Bell United Tel.	August 1981 September 1982
Kansas	Optional	Southwestern Bell	October 1984
Kentucky	Optional	South Central Bell	January 1, 1984
Louisiana	Optional	South Central Bell	December 16, 1983
Maine	No	New England Tel.	
Maryland	Optional	C&P Telephone	January 1, 1984
Massachusetts	Experimental (one town)	New England Tel.	November 9, 1983
Michigan	No	Michigan Bell	
Minnesota	Optional	Northwestern Bell	January 1, 1984
Mississippi	Optional	South Central Bell	July 13, 1980
Missouri	Optional	Southwestern Bell	January 1, 1984
Montana	Optional	Mountain Bell	February 7, 1984
North Carolina	Experimental	Southern Bell	January 1, 1984
North Dakota	Optional	Northwestern Bell	January 3, 1982
Nebraska	Optional	Northwestern Bell	January 1, 1984
New Hampshire	Optional	New England Tel.	January 1, 1983
New Jersey	Optional	New Jersey Bell	October 1983
New Mexico	Optional	Mountain Bell	February 1979
New York	Optional	New York Telephone	December 31, 1983
New York City	Mandatory	New York Telephone	Historical
Nevada	Optional	Nevada Bell	July 11, 1983
	Optional	Central Bell	May 26, 1983
Ohio	Optional	Cincinnati Bell	July 27, 1982
	Optional	Ohio Bell	January 31, 1982
Oklahoma	No	Southwest Bell	

Table 5.3: Local Measured Service Scorecard (Continued)

State	Status	Company	Effective Date
Oregon	Optional	Pacific NW Bell	Historical
Pennsylvania	Optional	Pennsylvania Bell	December 30, 1983
Rhode Island	Optional	New England Tel.	May 1983
South Carolina	Optional	Southern Bell	January 1, 1984
South Dakota	Optional	Southwestern Bell	January 1, 1984
Tennessee	Optional	South Central Bell	January 5, 1984
Texas	No	Southwest Bell	
Utah	No	Mountain Bell	
Vermont	Experimental	New England Tel.	October 1984
Virginia	Optional	C&P Telephone	November 1983
Washington	Optional	Pacific Northwest	August 1, 1981
		United Tel	July 9, 1984
West Virginia	Optional	C&P Telephone	January 1984
Wisconsin	No	Wisconsin Bell	
Wyoming	Optional	Mountain Bell	March 26, 1981

ten tying up central office switching capacity and local lines for several hours or days at a time at no charge to themselves beyond the monthly flat fee. Phone companies claim that data use of the public-switched system is increasing at a rate of about 20% a year. Consumer groups argue that residential users should not be penalized for this but that instead, the data users should be charged for data transmission as a separate class of service.

On the local level, in addition to Local Measured Service, the FCC CALC is another prime example of unbundling (though critics argue that here it is more than simple unbundling, since it is shifting a charge to consumers that they say should be shared by the long-distance companies). So also are telephone installation rates. Installation costs were once folded into the cost of the telephone, which was then included in the rate base as a capital asset. (Remember that the rate of return—profit—is determined as a percentage of the rate base. See Chapter 1). When the market for the sale of telephones became competitive, the costs were unbundled and installation was charged directly as a cost of service. Installing a telephone in New York, for example, now costs customers as much as $98.20. In 1970, the charge was $10.

Local unbundling has also been applied with the introduction of charges for directory assistance in most communities, a service that until recently had been free (that is, paid for by pooling basic service charges).

Proponents of unbundling say that it is good economics: it reduces waste that occurs when something appears to be free. They also argue that it is fair since only those who use a service pay for it. Opponents say it can be used for competitive advantage rather than for fairness to customers, and that the phone system is so complex that outsiders can't verify what the Bell companies claim are its real costs in providing each component of service.

In long-distance, a prime instance of unbundling is the recent decision by the FCC to permit AT&T to charge 50 cents for long-distance directory-assistance calls (on the grounds that that is what it will cost AT&T to provide that service). Other examples of unbundling include a separate charge for person-to-person calls and a charge for credit card calls recently adopted by AT&T. (Previously AT&T charged higher per-minute rates for these calls.)

DEPRECIATION

Another significant factor in the repricing phenomenon is the pressure for more rapid depreciation of telephone company plant and equipment. As a result of more rapid technological advances in the industry in recent years (such as digital switching equipment for data transmission and more cost-effective transmission of voice), telephone plant and equipment needs to be replaced more rapidly. Competition makes it necessary to have the latest equipment because companies with such equipment can operate more cost-effectively and offer more attractive services. The OCCs have been ahead of AT&T, primarily because the OCCs, starting business over the last decade, naturally purchased the most up-to-date equipment on the market. Here Bell has some catching up to do, since its equipment was installed over several decades.

To appreciate how the installation of new equipment affects pricing, it is necessary to review how depreciation works in the telephone industry.

Rate of Return and Reimbursement

Your telephone bill is essentially comprised of two elements. One is the rate of return the telephone company is allowed to earn on its investment in equipment (or plant) needed to provide telephone service. The other is reimbursement for the expenses the telephone company incurs in providing that service (cost of service). The latter element allows the company to cover its operating expenses; the former allows it to earn a fair profit. The regulatory scheme is designed to approximate a free-market situation in which consumer prices normally include the cost of operation (heat, light, salaries, equipment investment) plus a profit for ownership.

If a telephone company purchases a piece of capital equipment (let's call it a lathe) for $100, it cannot immediately pass along the cost of that equipment to users on a dollar-for-dollar basis. Instead, it must depreciate that lathe over its useful life. This $100 lathe might be depreciated over 10 years so that after one year its net book value would be $90; after five years, $50; and after 10 years, zero. (Once the net book value is zero, the telephone company has more of an incentive to replace the item since it can earn no rate of return on it.)

The net book value of the lathe is part of the rate base upon which the company's rate of return (profit) is based. The amount by which the lathe is depreciated each year is an expense (cost of doing business) and subject to reimbursement by ratepayers. Thus, assuming depreciation as described above, and a 10% rate of return, after one year the telephone company would be entitled to 10% of $90 ($9) profit (rate of return), plus $10 reimbursement for annual depreciation expense.

Now assume a longer depreciation schedule—e.g., 20 years instead of 10. After the first year, the lathe's net book value will be $95, and thus the telephone company will earn a $9.50 profit (compared to only $9 on a 10-year depreciation schedule). Note, however, that although their profits will be increased under the longer depreciation schedule, they will get only $5 reimbursement for depreciation expenses, and thus their cash on hand will be less.

Traditionally, the telephone industry, companies and regulators, have opted for longer depreciation schedules, lower rates and increased profits rather than shorter depreciation schedules, higher rates and increased cash-flow.

Rapid Depreciation

But now, because of rapid technological innovation and the competition it spawns, telephone companies are seeking permission from the FCC to depreciate plant and equipment more rapidly. In November 1980, in response to such requests, the FCC changed the way depreciation is calculated. It adopted a straight-line, remaining-life method, which permits the telecommunications industry to recover fully its investment in plant and equipment over its useful life.

As can be seen from our lathe example, rapid depreciation lowers net book value but raises immediate costs to ratepayers. Assuming a 10% rate of return and a 10-year depreciation schedule, our $100 lathe will cost consumers $19 after 1 year ($9 rate of return plus $10 depreciation expense).

Assuming the same rate of return and a 20-year depreciation schedule, our $100 lathe will cost consumers only $14.50 after 1 year ($9.50 rate of return plus $5 depreciation expense).

This method for faster capital recovery has resulted in approximately $3 billion in depreciation expenses since 1980. To recover those expenses, the Bell companies have been seeking higher telephone rates from state regulators.

For the most part, divestiture itself does not have direct impact on the depreciation issue. Although the divestiture entails a transfer of some $7.5 billion in BOC assets (e.g., customer premises equipment and equipment used for inter-LATA calls within states), AT&T has not requested significant changes in depreciation rates on such equipment. The one exception is on some $1 billion in intrastate toll-calling equipment in cross-bar offices. (Cross bar refers to a type of switching equipment.) Technological advances in this kind of equipment have been more rapid than those in equipment for switching local calls. When such toll cross-bar equipment was owned by the BOCs, it was combined with local switching equipment, thus receiving a lower depreciation rate. Now that it will be separated from it and owned by AT&T, AT&T has requested in 16 states that the FCC allow more rapid depreciation on it. The result could be higher rates in those states for inter-LATA calls within the state (even though AT&T is proposing lower rates for interstate calls).

On the whole, however, even apart from divestiture, the BOCs are expected to seek more rapid depreciation whenever possible. Experts anticipate that over the next three to five years the results of such depreciation requests, if granted, could add a few dollars more per month to the local bill—possibly as much as the FCC access charge.

6

Life After Divestiture: Functioning in the New Telecommunications Environment

One thing is certain—with divestiture and the restructuring of the telephone industry, all telephone customers, residential and business, are having to learn to deal with their telephones differently.

Before divestiture, with a single telephone call to an AT&T local business office, one could obtain all the telephone services and equipment one would need. Phone style and color, type of service and even long-distance–related services could be requested from that office, and a service person would appear at the door in a matter of days to install the telephones, make the repairs or whatever. A single bill came, which rarely told what the customer was paying for, other than "Service and Equipment."

One of the major consequences of weaning customers from Ma Bell is that they will have to make more decisions for themselves. Telephone servicing and shopping since divestiture has become much more complicated. The benefits will be found in more choice, greater competition and—the government hopes—lower prices.

But for most customers, the array of choices and services is viewed as an unfortunate, time-consuming chore rather than an opportunity. For the typical residential consumer, the changes in telephone service mean increased costs for the same basic service, with much less convenience. And typical small-business users may well find themselves in the same situation.

APPROACHING THE MAZE OF CHOICES

Bemoaning the additional hassles of dealing with the restructured telephone company may be a favorite pastime, but it is much like complaining

73

about the weather—there is no changing what has happened. Consumers, in whose name the changes in pricing and industry structure have been and are being made, need to make the best of the situation by understanding the new system and options available to them.

The first step in understanding the new system, services and options is to divide them into two more manageable categories: 1) choices in services and 2) choices in equipment. In each area, precipitous or uninformed choices can be very costly—as can procrastination because of uncertainty or confusion. Research and careful decision making, however, can save the customer substantial amounts of money.

Local Service Options

The public switched telephone network is at the core of local telephone service. Running a line from a central office to a home or an office, then switching and delivering local calls, are the primary functions of the local BOC telephone company in the post-divestiture era. And for all customers who want to make local calls, eventually they have to use the services of the local BOC. Local service is still a monopoly.

So it might not be surprising that it is the cost of local service that is increasing most rapidly. The FCC access fee for businesses became effective in June 1984, up to $6.00 per line after the first line. While states have approved only a fraction of the amount of the requested rate increases sought by BOCs, nevertheless, local customers are typically experiencing close to a 50% increase in the cost of local service. With unbundling of charges, sizable fees are being charged for services that used to be provided at nominal costs.

Local Calling Plans

One BOC response to the rising cost of local service has been to develop optional calling plans, primarily for residential consumers. These plans provide ranges in price based primarily on the number of calls placed by a consumer during a month. While these plans differ from state to state, the following is a listing and brief description of the most prevalent local calling plans:

- Flat-rate service is the traditional billing plan for most residential customers. A single monthly flat rate permits an unlimited number of outgoing local calls. This plan is ideal for heavy residential users of local telephone service.

- Message rate service, as offered in most states, permits a limited number of outgoing calls for a set, but lower, monthly fee. All calls in excess of the fixed number are charged at a per-call rate. For example, the monthly fee might be eight dollars, two dollars less than flat rate, with an allowance of up to 60 calls, and all calls in excess of 60 billed at 8 cents per call.

- Budget rate service is also often referred to as economy rate service. In some states budget service is just like message rate, except that the monthly fee is less and there are fewer calls allowed before the per-call charge is made. In other states, the monthly budget fee is very low, and there is a per-call fee for all outgoing calls.

- Local measured service is also referred to as optional measured service and is available in about half the states. Under this plan, there is a small monthly service fee, and each call is charged based on four elements:

  1. Distance—the rate will vary depending upon the distance of the place called. In most states there are usually only two calling bands, with the cost to call from one band to the other higher than calls within a single band.

  2. Duration—there will be a charge per minute of conversation, just like long-distance.

  3. Time of day—the per-minute rate varies with the time of day the call is made. There are discounts for calling during off-peak periods; again, just like long-distance.

  4. Unit charge—the cost of the first minute of the call usually contains an extra or unit charge on the theory that just hooking into the local system imposes certain nonrecurring costs.

Custom Calling Options

In addition to different calling plans for basic local service, enhanced service options, generally known as Custom Calling, are available in most places from the BOC. These services cost extra and normally substitute for additional equipment or services. The standard custom calling options in most states consist of the following:

- Call waiting: If you are talking on the phone and someone else is trying to call you, a tone tells you that another call is waiting. You can put the first party on hold and answer the second call. This can be a cheaper alternative to getting a second phone line.

- Call forwarding: This option allows you to have your calls forwarded to another number, either to be answered by you when you are at a location other than your home or to be answered by someone else for you when you are away. This can provide an alternative to a remote-control answering machine, and can assure timely notice of calls received. It may also provide extra security when you are away from home.

- Three-way calling: This option allows you to hold a conversation with two parties at the same time without the use of a conference-call operator. It is not only a time-saving convenience when two other people need to be included in a conversation, but it can save a lot of money on the call.

- Speed calling: This is a convenience that allows you to set up a series of one- or two-digit codes in place of seven-digit local phone numbers or ten-digit long-distance numbers that you dial frequently.

There may be a discount if these features are bought in certain combinations. The features are a function of the local switching office of your phone company, not a function of equipment in your home. Many of them, however, can be performed by equipment available for purchase, and it is important to comparison-shop.

Nonetheless, custom calling services can be used by smart telephone users as a means of saving on the monthly telephone bill. Call waiting in particular can be used to substitute for a second line. For the small business, the savings can be considerable, since there is now a six-dollar-a-month access-fee charge imposed by the FCC, in addition to the monthly local fee for the line. Call waiting saves both the access fee and the monthly service charge. Even for multi-line businesses, use of call waiting on various lines could reduce the need for additional lines. Typically, the monthly fee for a telephone line, plus the access fee, could be as high as $15 to $20 a month for the business user.

Enhanced Calling Service Options

Some of the BOCs are experimenting with new local calling service options similar to the custom calling options. Like Custom Calling, these services would be offered through BOC switching facilities and substitute in most instances for equipment that could perform many of the same functions.

The names for these services will vary from region to region. Generically, they have been called enhanced services. In Pennsylvania, where they are offered on an experimental basis in 1984, they are called Executive Class Service. This service allows the customer to make use of the fact that the BOC knows from what number a call is being made. To use the service, customers must rent, for $3.00 per month, a box that tells them what number is calling their phone. The service options include the following:

- Number blocking: Consumers can predetermine that certain people may not call them by blocking those telephone numbers from calling their telephone. A blocked caller will reach a recording that says the party will not accept the call.

- Special ring: The box can be programmed so that up to three callers will create a distinctive ring, letting the consumer know who is placing the call.

- Selected call forwarding: Under custom calling, telephones can be programmed to forward all calls to another location. With this service, customers can select up to three numbers to be forwarded to another telephone while blocking the rest of the calls.

- Number identification: The number calling will be displayed so the customer can see if he or she recognizes the calling number before answering the phone. It also serves as a trace on all incoming calls.

- Last number dial-back: It permits the consumer to call back the last number that called, which is particularly useful when a customer is unable to reach a phone before it stops ringing.

Customers will be charged only for the services they actually use once they have rented the box. For example, to call back the last number that tried to reach you would cost 15 cents. For services such as the call blocking or distinctive ringing, for which the phone company must keep the numbers you select stored on a computer, you would pay from 3 to 25 cents daily for storage, and from 5 to 25 cents each time the service is activated.

Local Bypass Options

Tenants in a building, whether apartment or office, may be able to save considerable telephone costs by the purchase and installation of a local switched network for their building. Since the franchise for local service is normally limited to offerings that cross city streets and alleyways, there normally would be nothing to stop building tenants or a building owner from installing a computer switch and telephone equipment. (See the more detailed discussion of equipment options later in this chapter.)

Not all BOCs agree that tenants should have the legal authority to build a switched telephone network. Southwestern Bell, for example, refers to this practice as establishing vest pocket telephone companies. And in Oklahoma, an administrative law judge considering a Southwestern Bell petition, ruled in October 1984, that shared tenant services were an infringement on Southwestern Bell's territory.

Nevertheless, where it is permitted, consumers may save money by the installation of a Private Branch Exchange (PBX) within a building. This privately owned switch will place everyone in the building on a private network for calls within the network. Thus, all the internal calls are free, without the unit charge normally assessed for each call on a business line. Moreover, a PBX allows the customer to change telephone numbers from one office to another, reassign numbers to different people, move equipment and more without ever contacting the BOC. The result is major savings for the customer of the growing transaction charges of the BOCs.

For example, assuming that an office building has 30 different tenants, with an average of 50 telephone lines per tenant, and assuming an average monthly charge of $15 per line, including the $6.00 per month access fee, the monthly cost for telephone service in that building would be $22,500. A PBX alone would reduce the number of lines needed in the building by about 25%, resulting in a cost savings of $7650 each month. Moreover, each new tenant would be assigned a phone number by the building managers, not the telephone company, thus saving the BOC fees for starting service, which could amount to hundreds of dollars. Minor changes in service for a tenant, such as deleting a line, would be done at little or no cost, while BOCs are charging up to $90 for this kind of service.

Cellular Mobile Service Options

New technology in mobile telephone service is promising to revolutionize local telephone service. The service uses traditional radio frequencies and computer switching centers to create a wireless switched telephone network. Although the initial service is designed for use in automobiles, the service is soon to be available in homes and in portable units that can be worn or hand-carried.

The system works through a series of low-power radio centers located throughout a metropolitan area. Each center or cell receives and transmits signals from the mobile radios between the different cells and switches them into the local hardwire network. As a result, the user can make or receive a call with the mobile telephone just like a regular wired telephone.

As opposed to the basic wired network in which the BOC has an undisputed monopoly, there is competition in the cellular mobile service arena. Under FCC order, there will be two companies in each major metropolitan area offering cellular mobile service. One of the companies will be the local BOC. The other company will be one selected by the FCC through a lottery.

Cellular mobile telephone is a great convenience to the user, and it will end what has been a national shortage of mobile telephone service radio frequencies. But it is an expensive service. The prices will vary from city to city and company to company. In Washington, DC, one company charges between $2400 and $2800 to purchase a system for the car. The price includes installation. If the customer prefers to rent, monthly rental is about $90 a month.

The cost for using a cellular mobile telephone is also expensive. Using the proposals in the Washington, DC, area as illustrative, we find that the non-BOC company will charge $35 a month, plus 40 cents per minute. Bell Atlantic is charging $25 a month, and 45 cents per minute. Thus, in Washington, the least expensive cellular mobile service will cost at least $115 a month in service and rental charges, plus per-minute charges.

LONG-DISTANCE SERVICE OPTIONS

Divestiture, in combination with deregulation, has opened up a wide market of choices for all users of long-distance service. This is not particularly so for the roughly 40% of the residential and business users who even in

1984 had rotary rather than push-button telephones. Prior to divestiture most of the long-distance users with rotary equipment have had to replace their rotary phones with touch-tone phones—and pay the higher monthly cost of the touch-tone service—to be able to use the alternative long-distance networks. This limitation, as well as the need to dial a special series of numbers for each non–AT&T long-distance service, are gradually being eliminated as a result of the introduction of a new system called equal access (see chapter 5) and the opportunity for consumers to presubscribe to long-distance services.

Presubscription

Presubscription is the method by which telephone users get to take advantage of the equal-access opportunity provided to all of the other long-distance services. As long-distance companies receive interconnections with the local telephone operating company systems that equal those of AT&T, customers will be given the opportunity to choose companies other than AT&T as their primary long-distance company.

Whichever company they choose will be the company that carries all their long-distance calls when they dial 10 digits—the area code and number. Before presubscription, all 10-digit calls dialed on the home phone were carried on AT&T's network. With presubscription, if a customer chooses MCI, then all 10-digit dialed calls will be sent over MCI's network. It won't be necessary to dial the 10 or 12 extra digits previously required for such an OCC's calls, nor will it be necessary to have a touch-tone phone.

Once customers choose a primary company, they will still be able to use other long-distance carriers, including AT&T, by dialing only five numbers before dialing the 10-digit number. Each carrier is assigned a three-digit identifying number, which is used to dial up the long-distance company. But it will still be necessary to have an account with a long-distance company to use its service. The following are the three-digit numbers of the major long distance carriers: Allnet—10-444, GTE-Sprint—10-777, AT&T—10-288, ITT—10-488, MCI—10-222, SBS—10-888, U.S. Tel—10-333 and Telesaver—10-221.

Let's assume you presubscribe to MCI. Each month MCI will send you a bill for the cost of all calls made from your home through regular dialing. If you decide you want to use GTE-Sprint for a call, if you have an account with GTE-Sprint you would only need to dial 10-777 and the area code and number. Sprint would bill you for all the calls made over its network.

Presubscription is going to be phased in over a three-year period. You will be aware of when it comes to your area when you receive a letter from the local telephone company asking you to make your presubscription choice. The first notice will come about three months before the date on which the new services will take effect, and you will have until three months after the start date to make a choice. (A schedule for 1984, 1985 and 1986 implementation is shown in Table 6.1, at the end of this chapter.)

Consumers who do not make a choice during the time allowed are going to be permitted to stay with AT&T. In some parts of the country, such as California, the states considered plans that will assign people who didn't choose, to other long-distance companies based on a variety of criteria. However, all of these different plans were abandoned in favor of defaulting all of those who failed to make an affirmative choice to AT&T.

All presubscription choices made during the initial six-month period will be made at no charge to the consumer. All changes in presubscription will bear a $5.00 cost charged to the consumer by the local telephone company.

The first market to have the presubscription system was Charleston, WV, which converted to the new system on July 15, 1984. Presubscription is slated to be phased into most U.S. communities over the following 12 months—eventually becoming available to about 60 million phone customers by September 1, 1986.

Choosing Among AT&T and Competitive Services

If a residential or business user has not yet considered the options available in service and pricing from AT&T's competitors, the introduction of presubscription in that user's community is certainly the logical time to do so. (It is not, of course, necessary to wait for presubscription if you have or are willing to order touch-tone service and if, as is the case in most metropolitan areas, the OCCs are offering service from your community.)

The following overview of the suppliers of long-distance service can be used as a starting point from which to become familiar with the choices available.

The companies that now compete with AT&T in offering long-distance service fall into two broad categories: 1) Specialized Common Carriers (SCCs) which own and operate their own long-distance networks; and 2) the resellers—companies that lease long-distance lines in large volume from the SCCs and from AT&T's WATS system and resell the use of those long-distance lines in the form of long-distance service to their own subscribers.

The SCCs

There are only five SCCs that own and operate networks. (Because of the enormous amount of capital and lead time required to construct such networks, it is unlikely that any new long-distance networks will be started from scratch from now on.) These five companies are:

- MCI: the original and still the largest of the OCC operations, which opened up the market with its Execunet service;

- GTE-Sprint: originally known as Southern Pacific Communications until it was taken over by General Telephone and Electronics in August 1983. Its primary offering is called Sprint;

- ITT: offers service through its long-distance operation, called ITT Longer Distance;

- Western Union: offers service through its long-distance operation, called MetroFone;

- SBS: Satellite Business Systems, a company owned jointly by IBM, Aetna and Comsat, offers a long-distance service called Skyline.

Even after divestiture, AT&T dwarfs these competitors in terms of its volume of customers, but the balance is expected to shift gradually, especially after presubscription is in operation. The main advantage the SCCs offer over AT&T is lower prices.

Their disadvantages are some limitations in the scope of services they offer. For instance, the SCCs have concentrated their network construction around linking major metropolitan areas, so business and residential customers in smaller or rural communities may find that SCC service is not available. Also, unlike AT&T, the SCCs don't have operators to assist callers if they have trouble or wish credit for a wrong number. (If an SCC customer dials a wrong number, the customer has to remember to deduct it from the monthly SCC bill.)

The Resellers

A consumer can be virtually certain that any firm offering long-distance, other than AT&T or one of the five SCCs above, is a reseller. This category of long-distance company is a relatively new phenomenon, which came into its own when in 1981 an FCC order made it possible for those who purchased or leased WATS lines from AT&T to resell use of them. The order created an opportunity that was particularly attractive to entrepreneurs because it made it feasible to operate a long-distance network without the huge capital investment required to build one. Since then, many scores of companies—too numerous and changing too frequently to list here—have come into being.

Using a reseller's service is no different from using an SCC service (and after presubscription is in effect, no different from using AT&T's service) but certain additional limitations need to be considered before subscribing to one. First, not all resellers offer nationwide service; some offer service only for calling within specific regions of the country. Second, reseller networks vary in size. Some have much less capacity than AT&T or SCC networks, so users may be more likely to encounter busy signals when trying to use those networks. This is a particularly important consideration for business users. Third, not all reseller services are available 24 hours a day, seven days a week.

Because most resellers are regional operations, offering service from only one or a few areas of the country, the local Yellow Pages (under the heading Telephone Companies or Telephone Services) is a good way to find out which resellers offer service from your area. Most BOCs are also compiling lists of companies that offer long-distance services through their system. A call to the local business office might get you a copy of the list.

Criteria to Consider when Choosing a Long Distance Service

With the advent of presubscription, competition among long-distance companies is becoming fierce. With it, the array of service offerings and prices will be much like those that emerged with deregulation of airline fares. That means consumers can expect a Byzantine menu of specials, super savers with special qualifications and frequent changes in service offerings in response to the novel packages that will emerge among the competitors.

A classic example of this is the Reach Out America plan proposed by AT&T in a filing with the FCC on April 19, 1984. While aimed at the residential market, business customers can expect to see variations on this plan tailored for them.

The plan proposes that for a one-time fee of $10 and a monthly fee of $10, AT&T customers could make an hour's worth of long-distance calls to anywhere in the United States during night hours (11:00 p.m. to 8 a.m.) and weekends. The rate for additional calls during these times would be $8.75. And for $11.50 per month, subscribers would also get an additional 15% discount on top of the 40% discount that AT&T already offers to all customers during AT&T's evening hours (5 p.m. to 11 p.m.).

For the evening and weekend segment of the plan, therefore, AT&T has in effect introduced postalized rates. Just as consumers use a 20-cent stamp to mail a letter to anywhere in the United States, so AT&T customers would be charged at the same rate whether their call was to a destination 100 miles away or 3000 miles away. (Note, however, that for the evening hours, the traditional distance rates—rather than postalized rates—apply.)

Plans such as this can look good at first, but if a consumer is looking for the best deal possible, it will be necessary to compare offerings from the competition. Often this may entail sitting down with a calculator and pen and working out the actual cost per minute after taking into consideration all the fine print in each offering. For example, the new AT&T rate plan will not save money for roughly 30% of the users, and it may be more expensive than similar calls over competitive networks. To illustrate, let's first figure out how much it would cost per minute to use the new AT&T service: 10 divided by 60, or 16.6 cents per minute. Currently, one hour's worth of nighttime calling to areas within 100 miles only costs .151 cents per minute over AT&T. Nighttime short-distance calls over ITT cost 13 cents per minute, while SBS Skyline charges 14 cents per minute for a 3000-mile nighttime call.

For consumers not accustomed to making such comparisons for telephone service, the prospect can be confusing. The first step is to simplify the comparisons wherever possible. The following seven questions will help organize such research and tabulation:

1. What companies serve my area?—Not all long-distance companies provide originating service from every city. Although hundreds of companies now provide long-distance service, most communities are served only by a handful—eight to ten. Your local telephone company business office will have a list of companies that have signed up for equal access. The Yellow Pages will have listings under "telephone companies," and several consumer groups maintain lists.

2. Which areas do the companies serve?—With AT&T a caller can originate and terminate a call in any part of the nation—indeed the world. The SCCs also offer universal termination in the continental United States, but not all resellers do. Until just recently, only AT&T offered international service. But in October 1984, MCI started service to several European

countries, and GTE-Sprint announced that it would start service to Great Britain in January 1985.

3. Is there a service fee or minimum bill?—Most long-distance companies used to charge a monthly service fee, but with increased competition prompted by presubscription only a few now have such charges. A number of companies have a minimum bill requirement for each month. The customer will pay the minimum charge even if no long-distance calls are made in the month, but if the minimum is met, there is no charge in addition to the normal cost of the calls. Some companies offer service options that require one-time-only service fees. For example, AT&T requires a $10.00 payment to sign-up for its Reach Out America plan, which also has a $10.00 a month minimum.

4. What are the billing increments?—AT&T charges in minimum one-minute increments for long-distance. If a caller hangs up after, say, seven seconds, the call is billed nevertheless for a full minute. Some companies charge in fractions of a minute—for example, a tenth or a sixth of a minute.

5. Does the company offer a travel feature?—Can you use your long-distance service when you are away from home? This is an important question to frequent travelers. Most companies also charge more for calls made while away from home. AT&T, for example, has a flat charge for different travel features, such as a credit card call or collect call. Other companies charge higher rates per minute for calls made away from home. These charges can make a dramatic difference in your monthly bill, so be sure to consider them when comparing services.

6. What are the rates for your typical calls?—Rates and rate packages vary dramatically between companies. Factors such as the typical length of a call, the number of different calls, the time of day called and the places called affect what your monthly bill will be with a particular service. Consumers may want to develop a composite bill with representative calls and compare the cost of making those representative calls over different long-distance systems. And don't forget discounts. Several companies now offer prompt payment discounts, and discounts for heavy users.

7. Is the quality of the service adequate for your needs?—SCC's often have been criticized for the low quality of the calls. They argue that with equal access the quality problems will disappear. But different transmission methods will also influence how a call sounds. Also, different companies have reputations that vary from city to city. So, it is important to try out a

service as it sounds from the city you call from most often to be sure it is good for you.

CHOICES IN EQUIPMENT

The acronym for telephone and associated accessories is CPE—Customer Premises Equipment. CPE no longer comes automatically from the local phone company with the order for service. The customer will instead have to chose whether to rent or buy the equipment, and then seek out the best outlet to implement that decision.

Rental equipment will continue to be available from AT&T through its post-divestiture division known as AT&T Information Services (ATTIS). (See chapter 3.) On January 1, 1984, the date of divestiture, all CPE not owned by the consumer automatically became the property of ATTIS—a subsidiary of AT&T. In other words, all the equipment in the home or in the office that had been rented from the BOC became the property and the responsibility of ATTIS.

Although the BOCs are prohibited under the Modified Final Judgment (MFJ) from manufacturing equipment, they may nevertheless purchase equipment and offer it for sale at retail prices in competition with ATTIS. Thus both residential and business customers can choose to purchase or rent their telephone equipment from ATTIS, the BOC or any number of private vendors who sell telephone equipment.

Residential consumers have a number of equipment options. Telephones and accessories can be purchased from an AT&T Phone Store (formerly called Phone Center Stores), the local BOC, non-Bell retail outlets and a variety of direct mail sources. In fact, most BOCs are choosing not to set up their own retail outlets. Instead, they sell over the telephone. At South Central Bell, for example, the business office refers new customers to its phone sales operation.

In most cases, residential consumers will have to go to the store or outlet to purchase their equipment, and then install it themselves. ATTIS will deliver equipment in some instances, but there is a $40 charge if the home is equipped with universal jacks and a $25 charge if the phones are hardwired to the wall.

Business customers will usually be served by a sales representative from ATTIS, a BOC, another firm that sells business phone systems or a consultant that contracts to determine needs and purchase the equipment.

Both business and residential consumers who want wiring changes or extension outlets can, in almost all states, do the wiring themselves, contract it out or have the BOC send a service representative. Most inside wiring and extension installations involve simple operations well within the grasp of the average residential consumer or maintenance staff of a business. BOC installation fees can be very expensive and consumers should be warned to get a price quote before having a BOC or any service representative to their premises.

It is important to remember that the wiring and the equipment on your premises are the responsibility of two different entities. Inside wiring will be either the responsibility of the customer or the BOC. For residential users, the BOCs are offering the ability to purchase insurance. Actually, the cost of maintaining inside wiring had been made part of the monthly service charge, and consumers had no choice but to pay the charge. Now, as part of unbundling, consumers are being offered the opportunity to decline to pay the charge, about 35 cents a month in most places. In return, however, the customer must pay for repairs of any inside wiring.

For businesses, this dual responsibility can be frustrating and expensive. First, whenever equipment is rented or purchased, it will be necessary to coordinate the installation of wiring to serve that equipment. Since divestiture there have been reports of extensive delays because of a lack of coordination. In one instance, new equipment sat uninstalled for weeks waiting for the BOC to come and install the wiring. Sometimes it is difficult to know whom to call for service. For example, if office A has lines 1, 2 and 3 while office B has lines 1, 3 and 5, and you to want bring line 5 into office A— who do you call? Be sure you are right, because a visit by the wrong company will result in a hefty charge.

Sticker Shock

If a business or organization has not moved or expanded its operations for some years, it is likely to suffer the equivalent of sticker shock over the cost of starting up service and installing equipment when it does so. A typical case in point is that of Washington Independent Writers, a small nonprofit organization in Washington, DC, which in 1984 moved its office to a new location within the city. The organization had five local telephone lines at its former location and wished to have the same number in the new one. The cost quoted to the organization by AT&T merely to install the equipment to serve the same five rotary lines was $1215 and, if the organization wished to purchase, rather than to continue to lease its old five-phone system with four buttons per phone, the cost would be an additional $2439. All told, the bill would have come to $3654.

Washington Independent Writers, like other organizations with similar sticker shock, quickly discovered that there were other vendors who could supply its needs at a much lower cost. After considerable research and shopping, it found an independent vendor that supplied and installed a more advanced touch-tone system with greater capacity for growth at a cost of $1300. The savings is $2354.

The case above certainly illustrates the point that telephone equipment has become a major budget item. But it also illustrates that becoming familiar with the options available in the equipment market can mean substantial savings.

Criteria for Determining the Best Equipment Package

A business can get a handle on the dizzying array of options available in the booming telephone equipment market by first of all—even before the shopping begins—setting up three key criteria to guide it in its search:

1. Current communications needs—This includes the number of telephones it requires and the kinds of features necessary to function efficiently (e.g., intercom, conferencing, call waiting, call forwarding, etc.).

2. Foreseeable communications needs—Equipment that can adapt to a business's growth several years down the line may be far more cost-efficient than equipment that has to be replaced because it lacks the capacity to handle expanded volume or changing communications needs, such as the introduction of data transmission.

3. Advisability of purchase vs. lease—Prior to the FCC's deregulation of telephone equipment, the only way to get it was to lease it from AT&T. Old habits may die slowly, but purchase is now an option that should be seriously considered. In this respect, telephone equipment should be regarded in the same category as any other capital investment, and the criteria an organization uses in determining whether to lease or purchase in other areas can also be applied here.

Becoming Familiar with the Main Categories of Equipment

The familiar single-line telephone—the kind most common in the home—is the basic Model T of telephone equipment, even though its appearance has become more varied and flamboyant. However, for a business of any size, having more than a single line is almost always a prerequisite. For smaller businesses, the most common solution is to have a key set system.

The Key Set

The familiar telephones with a series of push buttons are the mark of the key set system. Each button usually serves to connect the phone to a separate local telephone line. In some cases, when the customer has fewer lines than the amount of buttons on the phone, some buttons are inoperative. The primary advantage of the key set system is that the same telephone can be used to make and receive calls on several different lines and, as an option, if one line is in use, an incoming call can be automatically switched to ring on another line in the system. An integral part of a key set system is the key set unit, a box of electronic equipment on the customer's premises that links the phones and their lines together into a single system.

The most common key set systems handle anywhere from 4 to 10 buttons, but it is possible to have several dozen lines within the same key set system by the addition of a call director—a kind of master key set with scores of buttons, generally monitored by a receptionist. The industry rule of thumb is that key stations are best with 25 lines or less.

The PBX

Once an organization reaches a size in which it requires more than 50 local telephone lines and a variety of special telephone lines such as WATS lines or tie lines, the Private Branch Exchange (PBX) should be considered. Technically speaking, the old-fashioned private switchboard (as opposed to those in telephone company offices), some of which are still in operation, are PBXs. But the term as used today ordinarily refers to minicomputers, also called smart switches, located on the premises of the business that uses them.

These smart switches control a wide variety of automatic features that once had to be provided by the company operator (who, for instance, had to be called to request an outside line). Telephones connected to a PBX system do not require a series of buttons (as those in key sets) to access a free line for making an outside call; instead, the PBX automatically switches an employee's phone to an open outside line when the receiver is lifted.

But automatic access to an outside line is only one of an almost unlimited number of features that can be built into a PBX. Some of the other common features available on most PBXs are:

- Long loops: the ability of the PBX to serve not only the premises at which it is located but also off-premise extensions as well.

- Least cost routing: the automatic routing of a long-distance call onto whichever of the customer's long-distance services is available to carry that call most economically.

- Conference calling: the ability to connect several telephones simultaneously.

- Automatic callback: if a party within the system calls an extension that is busy, the caller can push a button and hang up. When the busy extension is free, both phones ring simultaneously, in effect placing the call again automatically.

- Call forwarding: an employee can have all calls to his or her phone automatically routed to another extension on the system.

- Permanent extension numbers: when an employee is transferred to another office or another department, his or her original extension number can be assigned to the telephone in the new location, thus reducing the need for constantly updating internal telephone directories.

Centrex

If a company's telecommunications needs are complex enough to require a PBX, but if that company does not wish to become involved in purchasing, operating and maintaining such costly equipment, there is another option: Centrex. Centrex is a service offered by the Bell Operating Companies that provides fundamentally the same features as a PBX. The name Centrex is an abbreviation of central office exchange service.

In effect, with Centrex a business uses the local telephone company's switching facilities to meet the internal needs it would otherwise have handled through a PBX. With Centrex, there is no miniswitch on the customer's premises. Instead, each of the customer's telephones is connected by a separate line to a designated portion of the local telephone company's switch.

While the Centrex option has been a viable alternative to a costly investment in PBX hardware, the FCC's access-charge plan for business customers threatens to make Centrex much more costly. This is because the FCC views each Centrex line as a distinct business line, for which there would be a separate $6 monthly access fee under its access-fee plan. For instance, a company with 500 telephones on a Centrex system would be billed $3000 per month, while a company that has 500 telephones served by a PBX may require only 300 outside business lines—at an access-line cost of $1800—to serve the same number of telephones.

Because this ruling could cause chaos to companies that had been operating with Centrex before the FCC access-fee plan was formulated, the FCC has made a concession to these companies. It has ruled that any company that had Centrex installed or on order as of July 27, 1983, would be charged only a two-dollar access fee per line.

Most BOCs are developing new marketing strategies in an effort to keep Centrex as a viable service. In most states, the BOCs have entered into long-term contracts at guaranteed rates for Centrex service. Many large business customers find the price certainty to be a major incentive to stay with the service. In most states, the BOCs are also lowering basic rates for Centrex to offset the increased cost of access fees.

But the developing PBX technology is going to make it difficult for Centrex technology to remain viable for long. Indeed, a few companies are now offering PBXs for as few as two lines.

Handling Repairs

One of the sources of greatest consumer confusion and concern in the post-divestiture environment is in figuring out just where to go to get equipment repaired. In the good old days, a simple call to Ma Bell would result in assured response—since the phone company was responsible for all parts of the system. Now, if service is down, a consumer will have to determine where the problem lies. A mistake can be expensive. If a local operating company service representative comes to the customer's premises only to find the cause of trouble is in a telephone handset that the business or residential consumer owns, there is likely to be a charge for the service call, and the consumer will still have to go elsewhere to get the handset repaired.

If the trouble is with the telephone line—that is, the outside wiring connecting the customer's premises with the central office, or in the central office itself, the local BOC is responsible and will make repairs without charge.

If the trouble is with the phone—or in the case of a business with some other hardware in its system—responsibility for repair will depend on whether the equipment is owned or leased by the consumer. If it is purchased equipment still under warranty, the vendor is probably responsible for repair. If it is leased equipment, responsibility will be with the company from which the equipment is leased, be it AT&T or one of its competitors.

Determining the Cause of Trouble

For the residential consumer, a little detective work when there is trouble can pay high dividends. If a residential consumer has more than one telephone and the problem exists on only one phone, the odds are that the trouble is in the equipment. If it is on all phones and jacks, even after each piece of equipment is taken off the line and the line tested with working equipment, then the odds are that the trouble is in the telephone company line or in the central office.

If the consumer has just one phone and it is equipped with a jack, a borrowed phone can be connected to the jack to test the line. If the same trouble occurs with the borrowed phone, the problem is probably the BOC's responsibility. If the trouble occurs only when making long-distance calls, the trouble is probably on the long-distance company's lines or equipment. In each case, the consumer must contact the appropriate party for repairs:

- Local service repairs are accomplished by calling the number in the service area for repair or the local business office.

- Equipment repairs will depend on where the equipment is from. If it is from ATTIS, it can be called directly on one of its 800 numbers. Usually, the customer will be expected to take the leased or warranted telephone to an AT&T Phone Store. ATTIS also has a program that permits customers to send in equipment by United Parcel Service, collect, to AT&T. If the equipment is not from AT&T, it should be returned to the store of purchase for repair.

- Long-distance trouble can usually be corrected by getting credit for a bad call. If the bad connection is over AT&T's lines, a simple call to the operator by dialing "0" will get an immediate credit. The OCCs, however, require that you note calls that were "bad" on the monthly bill at the end of the month, and take a credit at that time.

Understanding and Paying the Bill

All the confusion surrounding the divestiture on January 1, 1984, no matter how great it was, did not compare to consumers' confusion when their first post-divestiture bill arrived. With each subsequent bill, consumers are getting angrier and more frustrated. What had been one of the most readable and understandable bills suddenly became a six- to eight-page overwritten, impossible-to-understand insult.

The bill format, however, is largely dictated by divestiture. First, there was no time after the divestiture was agreed to and the date set for implementation for the BOCs or AT&T to come up with new bills. Thus, AT&T was forced to enter into agreements with the BOCs to do the billing for them. And, indeed, Judge Greene specifically permitted local telephone companies to offer billing services to other entities.

Thus, at least for three years after divestiture, the BOC will bill for both ATTIS and AT&T Communications. During this time, the phone bill sent by the BOC will have four basic parts to it:

- BOC local charges, which include monthly service fees, fees for special services such as custom calling, installation charges and service charges, if any.

- BOC toll charges. Some calls made within a LATA may carry a toll. This is often found in LATAs that cover large geographic areas. These calls are listed separately on the bill.

- AT&T Communications charges are the itemized long-distance charges for calls made over AT&T's long-distance system.

- ATTIS charges for AT&T rental or purchase of equipment.

The question is often asked whether a failure to pay long-distance charges carried on a BOC will result in the termination of local service. Many think it would be unfair to deprive a customer of local service offered by one company based on the failure to pay another, unrelated, company. AT&T, however, entered into contracts with all of the BOCs that provide, in effect, for the BOCs to buy the long-distance bills from AT&T for a fee. The BOCs argue that since they own the debt, they are entitled to collect it just as if the money were owed directly to it.

The FCC, however, refused to permit the BOCs to file a federal tariff permitting the termination of local service for non-payment of long-distance charges. They said they would leave the question to the states.

Although AT&T has indicated a desire to have its own billing system, the BOCs are working hard to convince all long-distance companies to use their billing service. In certain parts of Southwestern Bell territory, for example, the BOC has begun billing for Allnet.

Most long-distance companies, other than AT&T, have made arrangements with national credit card companies. Thus, MCI customers can choose to have their calls billed over American Express, Visa, Master Card or their Sears card.

Table 6.1: Equal-Access Availability Information—1984

Actual Customer Cutover Date	Date Customer Asked to Make A Selection	City/State	Area Code and Exchange
7/15	4/12 (N)	Charleston, WV	304-342, 343, 344, 345, 346, 347, 348, 357
7/15	4/12 (N)	So. Charleston, WV	304-744, 746, 747
8/19	5/20 (B)	Minneapolis-Orchard, MN	612-540, 541, 542, 544, 545, 546
8/24	5/24 (N)	Alameda, CA	415-521, 522, 523, 769, 865
8/24	5/24 (N)	Carson City, NV	702-882, 883, 884, 885, 887
8/24	5/24 (N)	Silver Springs, NV	702-577
8/24	5/24 (N)	Virginia City, NV	702-847
8/24	5/24 (N)	Churchill Butte, NV	702-629
8/25	5/25 (N)	Denver Main CG1, CO	303-534, 572, 573, 571, 575
8/27	5/27 (N)	Mobile-Springhill, AL	205-342, 343, 344, 460
8/27	5/27 (N)	Mobile-Azalea, AL	205-431, 432, 433, 438, 690, 694
8/27	5/27 (N)	Atlanta Toco Hills, GA	404-321, 325, 329, 633, 634, 636, 320, 982,
8/27	5/27 (N)	Atlanta Courtland, GA	404-221, 223, 222
8/30	6/21 (N)	Indianapolis-Trinity, IN[d]	317-872, 875, 876, 871
8/30	6/21 (N)	Indianapolis-Melrose, IN[d]	317-631, 632, 635, 233, 236, 262, 265, 266, 267, 269, 432, 443
8/31	7/27 (N)	Houston-W. Ellington, TX	713-481, 484, 922, 929
8/31	7/06 (N)	Chicago-Dearborn, IL[c]	312-329, 661, 644, 645, 670, 822, 410
8/31	7/06 (N)	Chicago-Wabash, IL	312-353, 886, 987, 461
9/01	8/01 (N)	NYC-West St. CG2, NY	212-732, 791, 587, 406, 437, 676, 618

[d] Indianapolis-Trinity, IN - NXX 871 added (8/17/84) no customers in NXX
[d] Indianapolis-Melrose, IN - NXX 432, 443 added (8/17/84)

Table 6.1: Equal-Access Availability Information—1984 (Continued)

Actual Customer Cutover Date	Date Customer Asked to Make A Selection	City/State	Area Code and Exchange
9/01	8/01 (N)	Backbay CG1, MA	617-247, 421, 424, 437, 536, 638
9/01	8/01 (N)	Backbay CGO, MA[d]	617-266, 267, 236, 262, 353, 578, 579, 572
9/01	6/01 (N)	Philadelphia-Locust, PA	215-466, 557, 751, 854, 972, 977, 988
9/01	6/01 (N)	Philadelphia-Penny Packer, PA	215-545, 546, 735, 875, 893
9/01	6/01 (N)	Wilmington CG1, DE	302-421, 428, 429, 651, 654, 655, 772, 773, 774
9/01	6/01 (N)	Wilmington CGO, DE	302-571, 573, 575, 594, 652, 656, 658
9/01	6/01 (N)	Hackensack, NJ	201-342, 343, 394, 441, 487, 488, 489, 570, 646, 692, 836, 695
9/01	6/01 (N)	Clifton, NJ	201-340, 478, 546, 772
9/01	6/01 (N)	Baltimore-Liberty, MD	301-367, 466, 542, 578, 664, 950
9/01	6/01 (N)	Baltimore-Columbia, MD[d]	301-596-0000 thru 8999 629, 730, 748, 964, 982-1000 thru 1999, 995, 997, 621-3000 thru 6999 and 8000 thru 8999, 973, 992-0000 thru 7999 and 9000 thru 9999
9/01	6/01 (N)	Portsmouth-High St., VA	804-393, 396, 397, 398, 399
9/01	6/01 (N)	Norfolk-Bute St., VA	804-441, 446, 622, 623, 629, 667, 624
9/01	6/01 (N)	Washington-SW CGO, CG3, DC	202-453, 485, 646, 245, 252, 287, 382, 447, 475, 488, 479, 651, 655, 732, 863

[d] Backbay CGO, MA - NXX 572 added (no customers in NXX);
[d] Baltimore-Columbia, MD. - split NXXs

Table 6.1: Equal-Access Availability Information—1984 (Continued)

Actual Customer Cutover Date	Date Customer Asked to Make A Selection	City/State	Area Code and Exchange
9/01	7/07 (N)	So. Euclid Evergreen, OH	216-291, 381, 382
9/01	7/07 (N)	Westerville, OH	614-882, 890, 891, 895, 898
9/01	7/15 (N)	Detroit-Bell, MI	313-221, 222, 496, 961, 964, 965
9/01	7/15 (N)	Detroit-University, MI	313-861, 862, 863, 864, 341, 342, 345, 927
9/01	7/07 (N)	Milwaukee Aetna Ct, WI[d]	414-257, 258, 259, 475, 476, 453, 771, 774, 778, 256
9/01	7/07 (N)	Milwaukee-So. 26th St, WI[d]	414-643, 645, 647, 671, 672, 383, 384, 649
9/01	6/01 (B)	Minneapolis-Downtown, MN	612-338, 339, 341, 347, 371, 330, 349
9/01	6/01 (N)	Denver Main CG2, CO	303-623, 624, 629, 620, 628, 631, 639, 595, 592
9/01	6/01 (N)	Portland-Capitol CG1, CG3, OR	503-220, 225, 226, 228, 224, 241, 242, 295, 299, 721
9/15	8/11 (N)	East Houston, TX	713-458, 459, 454
10/20	8/01 (N)	W. 42nd St. CG1, NY[d]	212-221, 354, 302, 413
10/21	8/26 (N)	Dayton 22 223, OH	513-223, 226, 228, 229, 331, 443, 445, 449, 457, 461, 949
10/22	7/22 (N)	Jacksonville-Riverside, FL	904-384, 387, 388, 389
10/26	7/26 (N)	Salinas, CA	408-422, 424, 754, 755, 757, 758
10/27	8/20 (N)	Indianapolis (Fishers), IN[d]	317-842, 845, 849, 841
10/28	9/02 (N)	Columbus 221, OH	614-221, 222, 223, 224, 225, 227, 228, 229, 821

[d] W. 42nd St. CG1, NY - NXX 413 added (no customers in NXX);
[d] Indianapolis (Fishers), IN - NXX 841 added (8/17/84)
[d] Milwaukee Aetna, Ct, WI - NXX 256 added (8/17/84)
[d] Milwaukee-So. 26th St, WI - NXX 649 added (8/17/84)

Table 6.1: Equal-Access Availability Information—1984 (Continued)

Actual Customer Cutover Date	Date Customer Asked to Make A Selection	City/State	Area Code and Exchange
11/01	8/1 (N)	Portland-Capitol CG2	503-222, 227, 229, 243, 248, 790, 796
11/03	8/15 (N)	Avenue R., Brooklyn[c]	212-627, 339, 375, 376
Indefinite	Indfinite	Stevens Point, WI[c+]	715-341, 344, 345, 346
11/09	8/10 (N)	Oakland, CA	415-273, 448, 452, 464, 466, 840, 874, 893, 869
11/10	8/10 (N)	Holyoke CGO, MA	413-532, 533, 534, 536, 538, 539
11/10	8/10 (N)	Natick, MA	617-653, 655, 651
11/10	8/11 (N)	Madison Spring, WI[c]	608-262, 263, 264, 266, 267
11/10	8/11 (N)	Appleton, WI[c]	414-731, 733, 734, 735, 738, 739
11/10	8/11 (N)	Eau Claire, WI[c]	715-832, 833, 834, 835, 836, 839
11/15	8/15 (N)	Seattle Main CGO, WA	206-345, 343, 292, 346, 421, 625, 622, 991, 995
11/15	8/15 (N)	Seattle Main CG1, WA	206-223, 442, 447, 583, 621, 625
11/15	8/15 (N)	Seattle Main CG2, WA	206-326, 340, 344, 382, 464, 587, 624, 626, 994, 997
11/15	8/15 (N)	Seattle Main CG3, WA	206-467, 628, 682, 947, 441
11/17	8/18 (N)	Salt Lake Main CG1, UT	801-237, 350, 355, 363 364, 366, 321, 322, 328, 359, 521, 522, 524, 526, 331
11/17	8/18 (N)	Denver East CG1, CO	303-398, 399, 393, 394 333, 355, 377, 388

[c] a change has occurred in the customer select date from previous report.
[+] cutover in jeopardy

Table 6.1: Equal-Access Availability Information—1984 (Continued)

Actual Customer Cutover Date	Date Customer Asked to Make A Selection	City/State	Area Code and Exchange
11/17	9/17 (N)	Columbus 464, OH	614-460, 461, 462, 463, 464, 466, 469
11/19	8/21 (N)	Ft. Lauderdale CR56E, FL	305-561, 563, 564, 565, 566, 537, 398, 390
11/24	8/24 (N)	Buffalo-Elmwood, NY[d]	716-881, 882, 883, 884, 885, 886, 887, 644, 878
11/24	8/24 (N)	Whitestone, Queens	212-767, 746, 352, 670
11/26	8/28 (N)	Anniston, AL	205-236, 237, 238, 235
11/26	8/28 (N)	Huntsville, AL	205-532, 533, 534, 536, 539
11/26	8/28 (N)	Montgomery, AL	205-261, 262, 263, 264, 265, 269, 293, 832, 834
11/26	8/28 (N)	Monroe-Main, LA	318-322, 323, 325, 329, 362, 387, 388
11/26	8/28 (N)	Memphis, TN	901-362, 363, 365, 369, 794, 795, 797
12/01	8/31 (N)	Brockton, MA	617-583, 580, 584, 586, 587, 588
12/01	8/31 (N)	Providence Broad CGO, RI	401-461, 941, 781, 467, 785
12/01	10/27 (N)	Little Rock Capitol, AR	501-223, 224, 225, 227
12/01	10/27 (N)	Wichita Amherst, KS	316-261, 262, 263, 264, 265, 266, 267, 268, 269, 436
12/01	10/06 (N)	Upper Arlington, OH	614-488, 481, 486
12/01	9/01 (N)	Reno, NV	702-321, 322, 323, 329, 348, 784, 785, 786 788, 787, 789, 793
Indefinite	Indefinite	Romeo, MI	313-752

---

[d] Buffalo - Elmwood, NY - NXX 890 removed (repair code only)

Table 6.1: Equal-Access Availability Information—1984 (Continued)

Actual Customer Cutover Date	Date Customer Asked to Make A Selection	City/State	Area Code and Exchange
12/01	10/06 (N)	Ann Arbor, OG1 MI*	313-662, 663, 665, 668, 763, 764
12/01	09/01-10/01 (N)	Nevada/Centel*	702-291, 295, 297, 298 361, 362, 366, 367 368, 381, 383, 385 386, 387, 388, 389 399, 438, 451, 457 458, 459, 564, 565 641, 642, 644, 645 646, 649, 732, 733 734, 735, 736, 739 798, 870, 871, 874 875, 877, 878
12/02	9/21 (N)	Hartwell, OH (CIN)[c]	513-761, 821, 948
12/02	9/2 (N)	Pittsburgh CG1, PA	412-281, 288, 433, 434, 633
12/02	9/2 (N)	Pittsburgh, CG2, PA	412-562, 566, 232, 234
12/02	9/2 (N)	Pittsburgh, CG3, PA	412-261, 263, 227, 456, 471, 553, 391, 394
12/02	9/2 (N)	Pittsburgh, CG4, PA	412-355, 565, 765, 392, 255, 642, 644, 393, 855, 333
12/02	9/2 (N)	Phil-Locust CG3, PA	215-263, 564, 568, 569, 496, 636, 231, 686
12/02	9/2 (N)	Phil-Market CG0, PA	215-238, 574, 592, 597 625, 629, 829
12/02	9/2 (N)	Phil-Pennypacker CG0, PA	215-985, 732, 585, 786, 841
12/02	9/2 (N)	Baltimore CG1, MD	301-244, 659, 528, 962, 234, 576, 347, 539, 727, 962, 954
12/02	9/2 (N)	Essex, MD	301-682, 686, 687, 391, 574
12/02	9/2 (N)	Pikesville, MD	301-486, 764, 484, 653, 358

*Additions as of 8/17/84
[c] a change has occurred in customer select date from previous report

Table 6.1: Equal-Access Availability Information—1984 (Continued)

Actual Customer Cutover Date	Date Customer Asked to Make A Selection	City/State	Area Code and Exchange
12/02	9/2 (N)	Virginia Beach, VA	804-481, 496
12/02	9/2 (N)	Newport News, VA	804-872, 874, 877, 878
12/02	9/2 (N)	Petersburg, VA	804-732, 733, 734, 861 862
12/02	9/2 (N)	Morgantown, WV	304-292, 293, 296, 291
12/02	9/2 (N)	Parkersburg, WV	304-422, 424, 428, 485
12/02	9/2 (N)	Wheeling, WV	304-232, 233, 234
12/03	9/03 (N)	Gainesville, FL	904-371, 372, 373, 374, 375, 376, 377, 378, 392, 395
12/03	9/03 (N)	Miami GR35E, FL	305-350, 372, 374, 375, 381, 577, 579
12/03	9/03 (N)	Miami GR35F, FL	305-347, 358, 371, 373, 376, 377, 379
12/03	9/03 (N)	Oak Ridge, TN	615-482, 483, 574, 576
12/08	9/08 (N)	Cottonwood, UT	801-942, 943
12/08	09/28 (N)	New Albany, 94C IN*	812-892, 944, 945, 948, 949,
12/08	09/28 (N)	New Albany, 01T, IN*	Access Tandem
12/09	09/28 (N)	New Richmond, OH (CIN)c	513-553, 557
12/10	9/10 (N)	Daytona Beach, FL	904-252, 253, 254, 255, 257, 258, 239, 250
12/10	9/10 (N)	Pensacola, FL	904-432, 433, 434, 435, 436, 438
12/10	9/10 (N)	Boca Raton, FL	305-368, 391, 392, 393, 394, 395
12/10	9/10 (N)	West Palm Beach, FL	305-650, 655, 659, 820, 832, 833, 837, 838
12/15	10/20 (N)	Columbus 2323C, OH	614-236, 231, 235, 237, 238, 239

* Addition as of 8/17/84
c a change has occurred in customer select date from previous report

Table 6.1: Equal-Access Availability Information—1984 (Continued)

Actual Customer Cutover Date	Date Customer Asked to Make A Selection	City/State	Area Code and Exchange
12/15	10/10 (N)	Evansville Harrison, IN[c]	812-422, 423, 424, 425, 426, 428, 429, 451, 464
12/15		Evansville, IN	Access Tandem
12/15	11/10 (N)	Topeka Central, KS	913-232, 233, 234, 235, 295, 296, 354, 357, 379
12/15	9/15 (N)	Idaho Fall, ID	208-525, 526, 529
12/15	9/15 (N)	Island PK, ID	208-558
12/15	9/15 (N)	Howe, ID	208-767
12/15	9/15 (N)	Arco, ID	208-527
12/15	9/15 (N)	McKay, ID	208-588
12/15	9/15 (N)	Moore, ID	208-554
12/15	9/15 (N)	Robert, ID	208-228
12/15	10/10 (N)	Melrose, IN[c]	317-232, 239, 261, 263, 264, 633, 634, 636, 637, 638, 639
12/16	10/05 (N)	Newtonsville, OH (CIN)[c]	513-625, 827
12/16	10/21 (N)	Ann Arbor SE, MI	313-434, 472, 971, 973
12/17	9/17 (N)	New Orleans-Metairie, LA	504-831, 832, 833, 835, 838
12/17	9/17 (N)	Chattanooga, TN	615-265, 266, 267, 752, 755, 756, 757, 751, 642, 778, 950,
12/17	9/17 (N)	Jackson, MS	601-352, 353, 354, 355, 944, 948, 960, 961, 968, 969, 949, 359
12/17	9/17 (N)	Atlanta SS, GA[c]	404-252, 255, 256, 257, 843
12/28	9/28 (N)	Hanford, CA	209-582, 583, 584

[c] a change has occurred in the customer select date from previous report.

Table 6.1: Equal-Access Availability Information—1984 (Continued)

Actual Customer Cutover Date	Date Customer Asked to Make A Selection	City/State	Area Code and Exchange
12/28	9/28 (N)	Stratford, CA	209-947
12/28	9/28 (N)	Alhambra, CA	818-281, 282, 284, 289, 300, 308, 570, 576
12/29	9/29 (N)	Boise West, ID	208-322, 323
12/29	11/03 (N)	Toledo, OH[d]	419-240, 241, 242, 243, 244, 245, 246, 247, 248, 249, 255, 259, 442
12/31	9/31 (N)	Hollywood HA45E, FL	305-454, 456, 457, 458

1984 yr. end - 134 End Offices

---

[d] NXXs added (255, 259, 442)

Figure continues

Table 6.1: Equal-Access Availability Information—1984 (Continued)

Actual Customer Cutover Date	Date Customer Asked to Make A Selection	City/State	Area Code and Exchange
1/1/85	10/1/85 (N)	Visalia, CA	209-732, 733, 734, 627, 685, 739, 625
1/1/85	Unknown (N)	LaPuente, CA (GTE)+	818-330, 333, 336, 369, 961, 968
1/1/85	Unknown (N)	Santa Monica, CA (GTE)	213-319, 393, 394, 395, 451, 458
1/1/85	Unknown (N)	Long Beach, CA (GTE)	213-420, 421, 593
1/1/85	Unknown (N)	Westminster, CA (GTE)+	714-891, 895, 896, 898
1/5/85	10/5/84 (N)	Roberts RSS, WI*	715-749
1/5/85	10/5/84	Houlton RSS, WI*	715-549
1/5/85	10/5/84	Hudson CGO, WI*	715-386
1/5/85	10/5/84	Hudson 81T, WI*	Access Tandem
1/6/85	10/6/84 (N)	Richmond, VA Grace St.	804-225, 343, 344, 345, 780, 782, 786, 788
1/6/85	10/6/84 (N)	Washington, DC - Dwtn. CGO	202-272, 347, 392, 393, 626, 628, 638, 662, 783, 879
1/6/85	10/6/84 (N)	Somerville, NJd	201-231, 524 - 0000 thru 3999, 526, 685, 722, 725
1/12/85	---	South Bend, IN	Access Tandem
1/14/85	10/14/84 (N)	Hollywood, MA92C, FL	305-920, 921, 922, 923, 925, 926, 927, 929
1/14/85	10/14/84 (N)	Miami, ME32E, FL	305-324, 325, 326, 549
1/14/85	10/14/84 (N)	Memphis, MTCGO, TN	901-535, 721, 722, 725, 726, 728, 729
1/14/85	10/14/84 (N)	Paintsville, KY	606-789
1/18/85	10/18/84 (N)	San Jose 02 CG1, CA	408-291, 292, 293, 294, 295, 297, 298, 299, 491, 920, 925

*Additions as of 8/17/84
d Somerville, NJ - Split NXX
+ NPAs corrected from previous report

Table 6.1: Equal-Access Availability Information—1984 (Continued)

Actual Customer Cutover Date	Date Customer Asked to Make A Selection	City/State	Area Code and Exchange
1/18/85	10/18/84 (N)	Vallejo, CA	707-642, 643, 644, 646, 648
1/19/85	10/19/84 (N)	Albemarle Road, NY	212-282, 284, 287, 462 181, 183
1/19/85	10/19/84 (N)	Broad Street CGO, NY	212-744, 952, 248, 511 701
1/19/85	10/19/84 (N)	Broad Street CG1, NY	212-482, 825, 668, 902
1/19/85	10/19/84 (N)	Buffalo Franklin, NY	716-842, 843, 845, 846 847, 849, 852, 853 854, 855, 856
1/19/85	10/19/84 (N)	East 30th CGO, NY	212-532, 725, 481
1/19/85	10/19/84 (N)	Kenmore Place, NY	212-258, 338, 377, 434
1/19/85	10/19/84 (N)	Varick St., NY	212-925, 226, 334, 431, 219
1/19/85	10/19/84 (N)	West 36th St., NY	212-239, 563, 971, 947, 560, 613, 502
1/19/85	10/19/84 (N)	West St. CG4, NY	212-608, 815
1/20/85	10/20/84 (N)	Boise Main CGO, ID	209-334, 338, 342, 343, 383, 385, 386
1/20/85	10/20/84 (N)	Star, ID	208-286
1/21/85	10/21/84 (N)	N. Dade County, FL	305-620, 621, 623, 624, 625
1/21/85	10/21/84 (N)	Montgomery-Normandale, AL	205-281, 284, 288
1/21/85	10/21/84 (N)	Birgmingham, WE92E, AL	205-923, 925
1/25/85	10/25/84 (N)	San Diego 12 CGO, CA	619-262, 263, 264, 266
1/26/85	Unknown (N)	Long Beach, CA (GTE)	213-424, 426, 427, 492, 595
1/26/85	12/17/84 (N)	Oklahoma City, OK-Central CGO	405-231, 232, 235, 236, 239, 270, 272, 278, 460
1/26/85	12/17/84 (N)	Springfield, MO-McDaniel CG1	417-831, 864, 865, 866, 868

Table 6.1: Equal-Access Availability Information—1984 (Continued)

Actual Customer Cutover Date	Date Customer Asked to Make A Selection	City/State	Area Code and Exchange
1/26/85	12/17/84 (N)	Springfield, MO McDaniel CGO	417-836, 862, 869
1/26/85	12/17/84 (N)	Kansas City, KS-Hedrick[d]	913-236, 3300 thru 3599, and 4000 thru 9999, 262, 281-6600 thru 6769 and 6780 thru 6899, 362, 384, 391-8200 thru 8299, 432 588, 676, 677, 722, 831
1/26/85	12/17/84 (N)	Wichita, KS-Murray CGO	316-681, 682, 683, 684, 685, 686, 687, 688, 689
1/27/85	10/27/84 (N)	Superstition Main, AZ	602-984, 986
1/27/85	12/24/84 (N)	El Paso, TX-Northeast CGO	915-751, 755, 757
1/27/85	12/24/84 (N)	Midland, TX-Mutual CGO	915-682, 683, 684, 685, 686, 687, 688
1/28/85	10/28/84 (N)	Orlando, MA72E, FL	305-723, 724, 725, 727, 729, 676, 768
1/28/85	10/28/84 (N)	Savannah B523A, GA	912-232, 233, 234, 235, 236, 238, 944
1/28/85	10/28/84 (N)	Baton Rouge, MACGO, AL	504-334, 381, 382, 383, 387, 388, 389
1/28/85	10/28/84 (N)	Chattanooga, DTCGO, TN	615-622, 624, 629, 697, 698
1/28/85	10/28/84 (N)	Habit, KY	502-729
1/28/85	10/28/84 (N)	Maceo, KY	502-264
1/28/85	10/28/84 (N)	Memphis, SLCGO, TN	901-332, 345, 346, 348, 396, 398, 922 601-342, 393
1/28/85	10/28/84 (N)	Nashville, MTCG1, TN	615-251, 256, 259, 741, 742
1/28/85	10/28/84 (N)	Nashville, MTCG2, TN	615-242, 244, 254, 255, 248, 252, 377, 885

[d] Kansas City, KS-Hedrick Split NXXs

Table 6.1: Equal-Access Availability Information—1984 (Continued)

Actual Customer Cutover Date	Date Customer Asked to Make A Selection	City/State	Area Code and Exchange
1/28/85	10/28/84 (N)	Nashville, MTCGO, TN	615-737, 747, 748, 749, 780, 782
1/28/85	10/28/84 (N)	Nashvile, STCGO, TN	615-269, 292, 297, 298, 383, 385, 386
1/28/85	10/28/84 (N)	Owensboro, KY	502-683, 684, 685, 686, 926
1/28/85	10/28/84 (N)	Pleasant Ridge, KY	502-275
1/28/85	10/28/84 (N)	Sorgho, KY	502-771
1/28/85	10/28/84 (N)	Stanley, KY	502-764
1/28/85	10/28/84 (N)	Utica, KY	502-733
1/28/85	10/28/84 (N)	Whitesville, KY	502-233
1/28/85	10/28/84 (N)	West Louisville, KY	502-229
2/1/85	11/1/84 (N)	Los Angeles 03 CG4, CA	213-620, 621, 687, 617, 976
2/2/85	11/2/84 (N)	New Dorp, NY	212-667, 979
2/2/85	11/2/84 (N)	East 30th St. CG1, NY	212-683, 684, 685, 460, 561, 576, 578, 696, 340, 686
2/2/85	12/24/84 (N)	Ft. Worth, TX-Edison CG1	817-332, 334, 870, 877, 878
2/2/85	12/24/84 (N)	San Antonio, TX-Fratt CGO[d]	512-651, 653, 654-0000 thru 2299 and 2500 thru 9999, 655, 656, 657, 650
2/2/85	11/2/84	Milwaukee, Broadway CGO, WI*	414-223, 224, 225, 226, 271, 278, 289, 347
2/3/85	11/3/84 (N)	Tucson Main CGO, AZ	602-620, 621, 622, 623, 624, 626, 628, 629, 791, 792, 880, 882, 884
2/3/85	11/3/84 (N)	Tucson - Mt. Lemmon, AZ	602-576

*Additions as of 8/17/84
[d]San Antonio, Fratt CGO Split NXXs

Table 6.1: Equal-Access Availability Information—1984 (Continued)

Actual Customer Cutover Date	Date Customer Asked to Make A Selection	City/State	Area Code and Exchange
2/3/85	11/3/84 (N)	Tucson - E. Benson Hwy., AZ	602-574
2/3/85	11/3/84 (N)	Albuquerque Main CGO, NM	505-242, 243, 247, 277, 765, 766, 841, 842, 843, 848
2/3/85	11/25/84 (N)	Cincinnati, CG1, OH (CIN)[d]	513-241, 352, 362, 397, 565, 566, 628, 629, 651, 684, 852, 950
2/3/85	11/25/84 (N)	Cincinnati, CGO, OH (CIN)[d]	513-381, 421, 562, 579, 621, 632, 721, 762, 763, 765, 977
2/3/85	11/3/84 (N)	Millburn, NJ*	201-376, 379, 467, 564
2/4/85	11/4/85 (N)	Orlando, PC 85E, FL*	305-826, 850, 851, 855, 857, 859
2/4/85	11/4/85 (N)	Charlotte, CGO, NC*	704-331, 336, 373, 374, 377, 378
2/4/85	11/4/85 (N)	Charlotte, CG1, NC*	704-332, 333, 334, 335, 337, 371, 372, 375, 376, 379, 570
2/8/85	11/8/84 (N)	Sacramento 02 CGO, CA	916-484, 485, 486, 971, 972, 483, 487, 489, 973
2/9/85	11/9/84 (N)	Manhattan Ave., NY	212-222, 864, 662, 678, 280, 316
2/9/85	11/9/84 (N)	Newton, NY	212-424, 426, 429, 476, 565, 639
2/9/85	11/9/84 (N)	So. Staten Is., NY	212-948
2/9/85	11/16/84 (N)	West 42 St. CG2, NY	212-395, 391, 398, 719, 382, 536, 419, 512

---

*Additions as of 8/17/84
[d]Cincinnati, CG1 CGO, OH - NXXs 352, 629, 765 DID - No Outgoing Service; NXXs 397, 565, 566-Official Cin. Bell Service, No Outgoing Service; NXX 684-Private Line Service; NXX 950-Feature Group B Only

Table 6.1: Equal-Access Availability Information—1984 (Continued)

Actual Customer Cutover Date	Date Customer Asked to Make A Selection	City/State	Area Code and Exchange
2/9/85	12/31/84 (N)	Kansas City, MO-McGee CG1d	816-221, 234, 247-1000 thru 5999 and 7000 -9999, 274-1000 thru 2999 and 4000 thru 5999 and 8000 thru 8999, 346-0000 thru 7999 and 9000 thru 9999, 374-2000 thru 7999 and 9000 thru 9999, 421, 471, 842
2/9/85	12/31/84 (N)	St. Louis, MO-Evergreen CGOd	314-261, 263-0000 thru 3999 and 5000 thru 6999 and 8000 thru 8999, 381, 382, 383, 385, 389, 553-0000 thru 6999, 679
2/9/85	12/31/84 (N)	Tulsa, OK-Elgin CGOd	918-560, 561, 581-0000 thru 6299 and 6500 thru 7999, 582, 583, 584, 585, 586, 587, 588, 592, 599
2/10/85	11/10/84 (N)	Billings CGO, MT	406-245, 248, 252, 259, 657, 256
2/11/85	11/2/84 (N)	Atlanta, PP89A, GA*	404-558, 676, 875, 892, 894, 897, 898
2/11/85	11/11/84 (N)	Florence, SC*	803-662, 664, 665, 667, 669
2/16/85	11/16/84 (N)	Broad St. CG3, NY+	212-785, 623, 482, 742, 480, 558, 440, 552
2/16/85	Unknown (N)	Del Ray, CA (GTE)	213-305, 306, 313, 827
2/16/85	12/21/84 (N)	Ann Arbor, CGO, MI	313-761, 769, 994, 995, 996
2/16/85	12/21/84 (N)	Ann Arbor SE CGO, MI*	313-434, 572, 971, 973
2/16/85	11/17/84 (N)	Neenah, WI*	414-721, 722, 725, 727, 729

*Additions as of 8/17/84
dKansas City, MO - McGee CG1 Split NXXs
dSt. Louis, MO - Evergreen CGO Split NXXs
dTulsa, OK - Elgin CGO Split NXXs
+ NXX codes changed from previous report

Table 6.1: Equal-Access Availability Information—1984 (Continued)

Actual Customer Cutover Date	Date Customer Asked to Make A Selection	City/State	Area Code and Exchange
2/16/85	12/21/84	Detroit Niagara CGO, MI*	313-343, 881, 882, 884, 885, 886
2/16/85	12/21/84	Detroit Tyler CGO, MI*	313-361, 894, 895, 896, 897, 898, 899
2/16/85	12/21/84	Mt. Clemens CGO, MI*	313-463, 465, 466, 468, 469
2/17/85	12/1/84 (N)	Kearns CGO, UT	801-964, 965, 966, 967, 968, 969
2/22/85	11/22/84 (N)	San Bruno, CA	415-583,588,589 872,952
2/22/85	11/22/84 (N)	Marysville, CA	916-742,743,634 741
2/22/85	11/22/84 (N)	Fullerton, CA	714-732,738,773 680,526,525 441,447
2/23/85	11/23/84 (N)	Syracuse State, CGO NY	315-421, 422, 423, 424 425, 426, 428
2/23/85	11/23/84 (N)	Syracuse State CG1, NY	315-470, 471, 472, 473 474, 475, 476, 477 478, 479, 480, 640 890
2/23/85	1/14/85 (N)	Houston, TX-Overland CGO[d]	713-680, 681, 682, 683, 686, 688, 956, 957, 895-1500 thru 1699, 939-3000 thru 3999 and 4500 thru 4599 and 4800 thru 4899
2/23/85	1/14/85 (N)	Houston, TX-Langham Creek[d]	713-463, 550, 859, 939-4000 thru 4399, 895-5500 thru 5699, 855
2/23/85	1/14/85 (N)	Houston, TX-Clay[d]	713-652, 657, 659, 751, 836, 976, 656-0000 thru 1099 and 1200-9999

[d]Houston, TX-Overland CGO Split NXXs
[d]Houston, TX-Langham Creek Split NXXs
[d]Houston, TX-Clay Split NXXs
*Additions as of 8/17/84

Table 6.1: Equal-Access Availability Information—1984 (Continued)

Actual Customer Cutover Date	Date Customer Asked to Make A Selection	City/State	Area Code and Exchange
2/23/85	1/14/85 (N)	Houston, TX-Mission	713-640, 641, 643, 644, 645, 649, 841
2/23/85	1/14/85 (N)	Ft. Worth, TX-Glendale	817-429, 451, 457, 496, 654, 930
2/23/85	1/14/85 (N)	San Antonio, TX-Pershing[d]	512-732, 733, 734, 735, 736, 737, 654-2300 thru 2499, 738
2/23/85	1/14/85 (N)	Ft. Worth, TX-Edgecliff	817-293, 551, 568
2/23/85	12/29/84 (N)	Toledo 53C, OH*	419-531, 534, 535, 536, 537
2/24/85	11/24/84 (N)	Phoenix Main CG1, AZ	602-226, 238, 255, 258, 259, 271
2/24/85	12/24/84 (N)	Lakeside Park, KY (CIN)	606-331, 341, 344
2/24/85	12/24/84 (N)	Shandon, OH (CIN)	513-736, 738
2/24/85	12/24/84 (N)	Norwood, OH (CIN)	513-396, 531, 631, 351, 841, 731
2/25/85	11/25/84 (N)	Miami, PB88E, FL*	305-883, 884, 885, 887, 888
2/25/85	11/25/84 (N)	Miami, PR66E, FL*	305-284, 661, 662, 663, 665, 666, 667
2/25/85	11/25/84 (N)	Coral Springs, CGO, FL*	305-344, 752, 753, 755
2/25/85	11/25/84 (N)	Atlanta, LA62C, GA*	404-622, 624, 627
2/25/85	11/25/84 (N)	Augusta, MT72C, GA*	404-722, 724, 821, 823, 828
2/25/85	11/25/84 (N)	Augusta, TH73C, GA*	404-731, 733, 736, 737, 738
3/1/85	12/1/84 (N)	Sunnyvale, CA	408-742, 743, 744, 745, 747, 752, 734, 756
3/1/85	12/1/84 (N)	Sacramento 03 CGO, CA	916-427, 424, 421, 422, 428, 391, 392, 393, 394, 395

*Additions as of 8/17/84
[d]San Antonio, TX Split NXXs

Table 6.1: Equal-Access Availability Information—1984 (Continued)

Actual Customer Cutover Date	Date Customer Asked to Make A Selection	City/State	Area Code and Exchange
3/2/85	12/2/84 (N)	Hoe Avenue, Bronx	212-842
3/2/85	12/2/84 (N)	East 37 St. CGO, NY	212-953, 883, 557, 972
3/2/85	12/2/84 (N)	East 37 St. CG1, NY	212-490, 949, 573, 599 370, 286, 808, 610 503, 983
3/2/85	12/2/84 (N)	East 56th St. CG2, NY	212-355, 644, 486, 521 759, 546, 308, 508 715, 605, 702
3/2/85	12/2/84 (N)	East 56th St. CG3, NY	212-223, 888, 838, 688 750, 906, 909, 980
3/2/85	12/2/84 (N)	East 56th St. CG4, NY	212-319, 751, 752, 310
3/2/85	12/2/84 (N)	East 167th St., Bronx	212-538, 590
3/2/85	12/2/84 (N)	Tratman Ave., Bronx	212-829, 822, 863, 430
3/2/85	12/2/84 (N)	West 73rd St., NY	212-362, 877, 724, 874 580, 496
3/2/85	12/2/84 (N)	West 176th St., NY	212-923, 927, 928
3/2/85	12/2/84 (N)	White Plains CGO, NY	914-285, 328, 335, 390, 391, 682, 683, 684, 686
3/8/85	12/8/84 (N)	Los Angeles 15 CGO, CA	213-298, 291, 292, 293, 294, 295, 290, 296, 299
3/8/85	12/8/84 (N)	Yorba Linda, CA	714-970, 779, 777
3/8/85	12/8/84 (N)	Sacramento 01 CGO, CA	916-322, 323, 440, 445, 449, 324, 328, 327, 321, 976
3/9/85	12/9/84 (N)	West Staten Is., NY	212-494
3/9/85	12/9/84 (N)	World Trade Ctr. CGO, NY	212-432, 775, 499, 912
3/9/85	Unknown (N)	West LA, CA (GTE)	213-206, 208, 209, 824, 825
3/16/85	12/16/84 (N)	Avenue Y, BKLYN	212-215, 332, 646, 934

Table 6.1: Equal-Access Availability Information—1984 (Continued)

Actual Customer Cutover Date	Date Customer Asked to Make A Selection	City/State	Area Code and Exchange
3/16/85	12/16/84 (N)	West 42nd St. CG3, NY	212-997, 840, 560, 921 944, 869, 556, 790 819, 930
3/16/85	12/16/84 (N)	World Trade Ctr. CG1, NY	212-466, 938, 321, 323 524, 839, 812, 616 480
3/22/85	12/22/84 (N)	N. Sacramento 11 CGO, CA	916-648,920,925 929,924,921 922,927
3/22/85	12/22/84 (N)	San Diego 06 CGO, CA	619-280, 289, 563, 584, 281, 282, 283, 284, 285
3/23/85	12/23/84 (N)	115th Avenue, NY	212-529, 843, 845
3/23/85	1/23/84 (N)	Hamilton, OH (CIN)	513-820, 863, 867, 868, 869, 892, 893, 894, 895, 896, 856
3/30/85	12/30/84 (N)	Binghamton-Henry, NY	607-722, 723, 724, 771, 772, 773, 774, 890
3/30/85	12/30/84 (N)	Buffalo-Main, NY	716-831, 832, 833, 834, 835, 862
3/30/85	12/30/84 (N)	East 56th St., NY	212-371, 593, 826, 750
3/30/85	12/30/84 (N)	Fairview Ave., BKLYN	212-326, 417, 821
3/30/85	12/30/84 (N)	Poughkeepsie Hamilton, NY	518-431, 432, 485, 486
3/31/85	1/31/85 (N)	Bethel, OH (CIN)	513-734, 735
4/6/85	Unknown (N)	Long Beach, CA (GTE)	213-432, 435, 436, 437, 491, 520
5/19/85	3/19/85 (N)	Warsaw, KY (CIN)	606-567
5/19/85	3/19/85 (N)	Glencoe, KY (CIN)	606-643
5/19/85	3/19/85 (N)	Groesbeck, OH (CIN)	513-245, 385, 741, 923, 972

Table 6.1: Equal-Access Availability Information—1984 (Continued)

Actual Customer Cutover Date	Date Customer Asked to Make A Selection	City/State	Area Code and Exchange
6/16/85	4/16/85 (N)	Evendale, OH (CIN)	513-243, 554, 563, 733, 769, 786
6/1/85	3/1/85	Omro, WI	414-685
	1st Qtr. 1985	158 End Offices	

(B) = Ballot
(N) = Notice

Source: AT&T

7

Conclusion:
Telecommunications Management

With the advent of divestiture and the repricing movement, the telecommunications environment in America has entered into a period of change that will be ongoing. Feeding this change are two forces:

1. The drive within the FCC, especially under the Reagan administration, to achieve almost total deregulation as fast as possible; and

2. the growing range of new services available from new technology rapidly coming into its own, especially in the business marketplace.

THE DRIVE FOR DEREGULATION

Despite the opening of long-distance service to full competition with presubscription, the long-distance industry remains dominated by one company—AT&T—which controls an estimated 94% of the market in which competition is possible. Because AT&T is such an enormous market force, AT&T's competitors—the OCCs—set their prices to compete primarily against AT&T rather than against each other.

Because of such market dominance—even after divestiture—AT&T remains much more tightly regulated than the OCCs. To change its long-distance rates or make a new service offering, for instance, AT&T must still receive FCC approval. It must still file tariff proposals with the FCC, allowing 45 days for public comment, after which the FCC can refuse to permit the proposed AT&T changes.

By contrast, the FCC has been progressively deregulating the OCCs, on the principle that since no OCC has anything near a dominant share of the market, none can control the market by predatory pricing or other pressures on the competition. Indeed, the FCC in October 1984, agreed to AT&T's request that it reduce the waiting period before AT&T tariffs can become effective from 90 days to 45 days. Next, the FCC totally deregulated the resellers, removing even the character requirements that had been necessary to receive a license to operate a common-carrier network. Then, in late 1983, the FCC authorized the OCCs to operate without tariffs, allowing them to change prices and rates whenever they wished.

As might be expected, AT&T has begun pointing to such deregulation as reason why it also should be deregulated, contending that OCC deregulation has given its competition an unfair advantage. It has introduced this argument, for instance, in its request to the FCC that it be allowed to implement its Reach Out America long-distance discount plan after a 45-day waiting period rather than the required 90-day period.

But even though the FCC claims that total deregulation of the OCCs is motivated by its desire to serve the public interest by stimulating competition, the OCCs did not withdraw their tariffs when given permission to do so in 1983. Their reason for caution: The OCCs see behind their own total deregulation a strategy by the FCC to set a precedent for total deregulation of AT&T, ignoring what the OCCs view as AT&T's continued market dominance. Their suspicions appear to have been confirmed by a subsequent order from the FCC that the OCCs actually comply with the options of withdrawing their tariffs.

In effect, the FCC appears to have a commitment to a total free-market philosophy closely reflecting the philosophy of the Reagan administration. Such philosophy is shown by its steadfast commitment to eventually implement its access-fee charge, targeting businesses to carry the burden of this charge if, as it has appeared, it will be politically unfeasible to apply it in the residential sector.

New Technologies

Competition in long-distance is not the only area in which revolutionary change is under way for telecommunications users. New technology is also revolutionizing the way telecommunications systems can be used. For a business, being aware of new technologies and taking advantage of them can mean the difference between keeping up with or moving ahead of one's competition, or being left behind in the dust.

Business consumers should be aware of three areas in particular that are rapidly coming into their own.

Electronic Mail

Companies such as MCI and Western Union have aggressively begun marketing this service, by which it is possible to send mail instantly anywhere in the U.S. All that is required to send such mail is a modem, which can be hooked up to any electronic communicating equipment, such as a personal computer, word processor, electronic typewriter, work station, data terminal or telex machine. Recipients can receive such mail if they have similar equipment or, if they do not, the electronic mail can be delivered in the destination city by messenger or the U.S. Post Office.

Rates for this service make it competitive with overnight mail, beginning at one dollar for three printed pages if the mail goes directly to the receiving party's electronic terminal.

Cellular Telephone

This new technology, using a series of microwave terminals located in a metropolitan area coordinated by a computer, makes it possible for thousands of callers to use mobile telephone service simultaneously; in the past it was technically possible only to accommodate a very limited number of calls. While still expensive, such mobile phone service offerings can now be cost-effective for many businesses. Rates range currently at about 40 cents per minute for local calls, plus a monthly service charge of approximately $35. Phones, including installation, run from $2000 to $9000 to purchase, but can be leased for about $90 a month.

Cable

Cable television systems, originally built to serve the entertainment market, are also capable of carrying telecommunications signals. As such, they offer the potential, still barely tapped, of interactive video services, such as electronic banking and other financial transactions from the home. In addition, as cable systems grow, they begin, in effect, to duplicate the copper-wire lines of local telephone systems.

In a number of cities, such as New York and Omaha, cable companies are beginning to compete with the local telephone company for private-line traffic, especially for direct transmission of data between two locations. As a result, the telephone industry is seeking in many states to regulate such cable company activity, just like telephone. Congress, however, has just passed legislation that permits state regulation of cable on a limited basis, and assures the right of local cable companies to provide certain data services.

For the near future, however, (except for use by very large organizations to bypass local telephone company systems) the telecommunications applications of cable remain bogged down in regulatory restrictions and in the cable systems' as yet limited scope of coverage in most communities. Nevertheless, cable is a sleeping giant—the technology to watch.

TELECOMMUNICATIONS AS AN EMERGING MANAGEMENT DISCIPLINE

In the new telecommunications environment, it is no longer safe to leave telecommunications in the category of management by afterthought.

Just as marketing and personnel policy have taken their place with finance and business plans as standard disciplines in the operation of modern business, so too, telecommunications management is becoming an area that businesses are well-advised to structure into their management systems.

This has been the case for some time with big business, where a telecommunications manager in a *Fortune* 500 firm can be responsible for a multimillion-dollar budget with a staff as large as that of a moderate-sized company.

But formal telecommunications management is also becoming a necessity even in smaller companies. The experience of sticker shock over the cost of new equipment and service described in chapter 6 illustrates why. Telecommunications is no longer an incidental budget item. And the new environment of ongoing change—both in the drive for total deregulation and in the rapid proliferation of new telecommunications technologies—further illustrates the need for systematic and sustained management attention.

As a business grows larger, it is well advised to consider creating a full-time telecommunications management position within the company. The return on investment in cutting costs and in achieving efficient service can often justify such a move. For companies that are not yet large enough to require a full-time telecommunications manager, the best strategy is to assign this responsibility as part of the job description of one specific person and to allow for the time and training (such as attending a telecommunications training seminar) for this person to become the resident expert on whom management can rely.

Whether the telecommunications manager functions in that role as a full-time or part-time position, this manager should be assigned the responsibility to develop a thorough and current working knowledge of the following areas:

- all long-distance suppliers serving the company's territories, including comparative charts on their service offerings and rates as they change;

- the range of equipment suited to the volume and nature of the company's calling needs, as well as determinations on which equipment will be most cost-effective as the company grows;

- local telecommunications vendors and telecommunications consultants—along with evaluations from other companies of the user's size that have used these vendors and consultants;

- developments in regulatory and legislative issues in telecommunications that are likely to significantly affect the company's costs or service options. The drive for deregulation puts telecommunications squarely into the political arena. Users must make their concerns known to their elected representatives if they expect to protect their interests; and

- a network of fellow managers in other companies in the community who have similar telecommunications responsibilities. Enormous amounts of research and learning time can be saved by developing or hooking into such informal networks. This group can also serve as a mutual back-up resource in monitoring new equipment and services as they become available. It can also be mobilized as a local lobbying group when an issue of mutual concern requires mailings or visits to elected representatives or to the FCC or state PUCs.

Appendix:
Telephone Industry Time Line

1958—Regulatory

The FCC in its "above 890" decision allowed the construction of private microwave systems above 890 megacycles. At the time, it was seen as relatively unimportant. However, this ruling opened the way to private networks that bypass the switched networks.

1966—Regulatory

FCC's Computer Inquiry I study was launched to determine the potential impact of the merging of computer and communications technology on the communications business.

1968—Regulatory

In the Carterfone decision, the FCC struck down prohibitive interconnection rules and allowed non-Bell equipment to be connected to the network using Protective Connecting Arrangements (PCAs).

1969—Regulatory

The first case of intercity (long-distance) competition was allowed when the FCC authorized MCI to connect and operate private line facilities between St. Louis and Chicago.

1970—Regulatory

In its Specialized Common Carrier ruling, the FCC established the desirability of competition in the intercity market but limited it to private line facilities. The Bell System argued that the decision was tantamount to market allocation and would result in cream skimming—allowing competitors to serve high-density, high-profit routes, draining off revenues used to subsidize basic local service.

1972—Regulatory

The FCC decision in Computer Inquiry I determined that there were distinctions between the computer and communications industries and that the computer industry was to remain unregulated.

1973—Regulatory

In a landmark address to the National Association of Regulatory Utility Commissioners (NARUC), AT&T Chairman John DeButts called for a moratorium on further regulatory activity in the telecommunications industry until the full implications of recent FCC decisions could be assessed. DeButts warned of serious problems with local rate structures and with the possibility of abandoning nationwide rate averaging if competition in the intercity market was to grow significantly.

1974—Judicial

The U.S. Justice Department filed an antitrust suit against the Bell System, charging conspiracy to monopolize the telecommunications industry. The Justice Department sought as a remedy the divestiture of Western Electric and the separation of the operating telephone companies from AT&T Long Lines.

1974—Regulatory

The FCC asked AT&T to postpone introduction of new Hi-Lo tariffs. This rate structure was designed in direct response to competition in the private-line long-distance business and was the Bell System's first departure from nationwide average pricing. Two years later, after study, the FCC ordered AT&T to submit replacement tariffs.

1975—Regulatory

The FCC barred MCI's Execunet service because it was more like regular long-distance service than private line. The FCC later reconsidered but finally ruled against Execunet in mid-1976.

1975—Regulatory

The FCC established a program allowing "registered" terminal equipment to be connected to the telephone network with no protective connecting arrangement. This program, which went into effect in 1977, is still in effect.

1976—Regulatory

The FCC opened Computer Inquiry II. Prompted by the general unpopularity of its CI-I order, CI-II was instituted to take another look at computer-communications issues.

1976—Regulatory

The FCC ordered unlimited resale and sharing of private line service.

1976—Judicial

The U.S. Court of Appeals upheld the FCC's jurisdiction over terminal equipment, pre-empting state authority.

1976—Legislative

The Consumer Communications Reform Act (CCRA), drafted with the help of the Bell System, was introduced in the House of Representatives. The bill affirmed universal service as a policy goal and set tests for competitors to enter the intercity and terminal equipment markets. Although the bill attracted more than 200 sponsors, it died in committee. A similar measure introduced in the Senate met the same fate.

1977—Regulatory

The FCC's Registration Program took effect. Registered terminal equipment could be connected to the telephone network without a protective connecting arrangement.

1977—Legislative

CCRA was reintroduced in both houses, but again, the bills died in committee. Nevertheless, reaction to the bills aroused congressional interest in the issue and led to hearings in both the House and the Senate on the need for change in national telecommunications policy.

1978—Judicial

The Supreme Court refused to review a Court of Appeals ruling that overturned the FCC ban on Execunet and ordered Bell to offer interconnection facilities to MCI. In effect, this ruling opened the intercity long-distance market to competition.

1978—Legislative

The House Communications Subcommittee introduced H.R. 13015—a rewrite of the Communications Act of 1934. The bill encouraged competition through deregulation and restructuring of the Bell System. Hearings were held, but the bill died in committee.

1979—Legislative

The House Communications Subcommittee introduced new legislation—H.R. 3333. After revisions in markup, the bill was trimmed down and reintroduced as H.R. 6121. The Senate also introduced two bills: S. 611 and S. 622; neither moved out of committee.

Nevertheless, legislation in both houses continued along a deregulatory, competitive thrust.

1979—Regulatory

The FCC endorsed an agreement reached in December 1978 between AT&T and other common carriers that provided the equivalent of long-distance telephone service. Under the agreement, the OCCs would pay Bell for the use of its local switches and lines used to complete long-distance calls. Known as the exchange network facilities interstate access (ENFIA) agreement, payments made under this arrangement were, in essence, access charges—a key issue today.

1980—Legislative

New legislation—H.R. 6121, revised again in markup—was approved by the House Commerce Committee. The bill stalled in the Judiciary Committee's review and died with the end of the congressional session.

The Senate merged S. 611 and S. 622 into S. 2827; that bill also died with the session.

1980—Regulatory

The FCC issued its final order in Computer Inquiry II. The order detariffed enhanced services and terminal equipment and required that

Bell set up a separate subsidiary if it wished to offer such services after January 1, 1983.

1981—Judicial

Hearings began in the Justice Department's antitrust suit against the Bell System.

1981—Legislative

New legislation—Senate bill S. 898—was introduced and later passed by a 90-4 vote.

1981—Legislative

The House Telecommunications Subcommittee introduced yet another new piece of legislation—H.R. 5158, its version of a redefined national telecommunications policy. The bill was abandoned by Rep. Timothy Wirth, its chief sponsor, in July 1982.

1982—Judicial

The Justice Department and AT&T on January 8 announced an agreement in the seven-year-old antitrust case against the Bell System. The agreement called for AT&T to divest itself of its 22 wholly owned local Bell Operating Companies. Those companies would be allowed to form seven regional companies, separate and independent from one another. After public hearings, Federal Judge Harold Greene, the presiding judge in the antitrust case, approved the Modification of Final Judgment (MFJ)—as it is called—on August 24, 1982. In the next major step toward divestiture, AT&T filed its Plan of Reorganization (POR) on December 16, 1982.

1983—Judicial

Judge Greene basically approved the Plan of Reorganization on July 8—18 months after the agreement was first announced—and sought six changes.

On August 3, AT&T accepted the last few court-proposed modifications—the latest milestone in the episodic and often dramatic unfolding of the events leading up to the divestiture in January 1984.

Glossary of Telecommunications Terminology

Access: The capability to enter the local, nationwide and international networks, which, in turn, gives the user the ability to reach or communicate with someone else. From a customer's perspective, access is the ability to communicate with the outside world. From an interexchange carrier's perspective, access is the ability to reach all telephones in a geographic area.

Access charge: A tariff imposed on either end-users or interexchange carriers to compensate the Bell Operating Company (BOC) for the origination and termination of calls, that is, the connections between end-users and inter-LATA carriers (ICs) via BOC-provided facilities. This charge will be used in place of the present Exchange Network Facilities for Interstate Access (ENFIA tariff charges and the Division of Revenues process).

Access-charge tariffs: These tariffs were filed in accordance with the Modification of Final Judgment (MFJ) and the FCC's access-charge order in CC-Docket 78–72. Set forth in these tariffs are the terms, conditions, rate structures and rates related to the use of exchange access facilities, as provided by the Bell Operating Companies (BOCs), for originating and terminating inter-LATA telecommunications by all inter-LATA carriers. The tariffs will include both direct end-user charges and carrier charges (pooled and averaged) for non–traffic-sensitive (NTS) plant during a seven-year transition to full end-user charges.

127

Access costs: Access costs consist of two broad categories—a category encompassing costs that do not vary with usage volumes (fixed costs) and a category encompassing costs that vary with usage. The fixed, or non–traffic-sensitive (NTS) component represents the costs of connecting a customer's access line to a Bell Operating Company's (BOC's) end office. It includes such items as the subscriber loop, the drop line, and for the present, the inside wiring and the customer's telephone. These fixed access costs occur whether a customer uses the telephone or not. The usage-sensitive category of access costs represents the costs of the switching and trunking equipment required to transport a call from an end office to the interexchange carrier or vice versa. The amount of equipment required is sensitive to the volume of calls (traffic) generated by the many customers who share this equipment.

Access line: The facilities between a serving central office and the customer that are required to provide access to the local and toll switched network with the exception of dedicated facilities such as a private line. The access line currently includes the non–traffic-sensitive (NTS) central office equipment, the subscriber loop, the drop line, inside wiring and the main jack. Access-line costs are fixed costs and are incurred by virtue of subscription to telephone service.

Bypass: Use of alternative distribution arrangements in order to avoid the local telephone company network. Facilities such as cellular radio, two-way cable TV, short-haul microwave and direct satellite to rooftop antennas are examples of technological developments being employed by Other Common Carriers (OCCs) and cable TV companies that have the capability to circumvent the use of the local telephone network. The existence of these alternatives is a major consideration in the development of access charges.

Central office: The telephone company location that serves a specific geographical area by having all customer telephone wires terminate at that place. Also the switch at a central office acts as a concentrator to allow fewer outgoing trunks (those lines that connect with the rest of the network) to serve a greater number of customers.

Central services organization (CSO): The post-divestiture organization that is responsible for the provision of centralized technical and management services and various administrative functions for the Regional Bell Operating Telephone Companies (BOCs). It serves as the single point of contact for government communications associated with national security and emergency preparedness.

Common carrier: A supplier in an industry that undertakes to carry goods, services or people from one point to another for the public in general or for specified classes of the public. In telecommunications, such carriage related to provision of a telecommunications network. A common-carrier company that offers communications services to the public is subject to regulation by federal and state commissions.

Customer access line charge (CALC): A monthly charge associated with a residence or business line paid by the end-user in order to recover a portion of the non–traffic-sensitive (NTS) costs. The CALC may have two components: one that is fixed and one that varies with usage.

Customer premises equipment (CPE): All telecommunications terminal equipment located on the customer premises, both state and interstate, except coin-operated telephones, and encompassing everything from black telephones to the most advanced data terminals and private Branch Exchanges (PBXs). Under the CI-II order, embedded CPE, i.e., CPE installed or in Bell Operating Company (BOC) inventories prior to January 1, 1983, will continue to be provided by the BOCs under tariff for an interim period. New CPE will not be tariffed and may be provided only through a separate subsidiary.

Depreciation: An accounting procedure used to set aside the difference between the first cost for an item of plant (capital) and its estimated net salvage at the end of its expected life. This amount to be depreciated is treated as an expense to offset revenues for tax purposes over the years of expected life.

Division of revenues (DR): The means by which Bell System Companies that furnished interstate services shared in the revenues from these services. Under this plan, each company was first reimbursed for expenses (including taxes) incurred in rendering the service, and then each company shared in the balance of interstate revenues in proportion to the amount of investment devoted to interstate business. The 1982 Consent Decree required that, upon divestiture, this process be replaced with a system of access charges.

Exchange Network Facilities for Interstate Access (ENFIA): This is a charge negotiated between AT&T and the Other Common Carriers (OCCs) in 1979, under which the OCCs now pay 55% of a calculated equivalent Bell System charge for accessing the local network.

Equal access: An unbundled Bell Operating Company (BOC) tariff offering Local Access and Transport Area (LATA) access, the first phase of which must be offered to all inter-LATA carriers starting no later than September 1, 1984. Such access must be equal in type, quality and price to that provided to the AT&T interexchange entity (AT-TIX) and its affiliates.

Exchange: A geographical area established by a regulated body for the provision of exchange telecommunications services. An exchange may be serviced by one or more central offices. This does not have the same meaning as the "exchanges" defined by the Modification of Final Judgement (MFJ).

Independent Telephone Company: A telephone company (not a Bell telephone company) that furnishes telecommunications service under franchise within a geographical area. There are about 1450 independent telephone companies ranging in size from the multibillion-dollar General Telephone and Electronics (GTE) down to very small independents with revenues measured in the hundreds of thousands of dollars. Those companies all share in long-distance revenues as part of the Independent Bell System partnership. This system will need to be redetermined after the final decision on the AT&T Consent Decree (1982). The independents as a group account for about 20% of the telephone customers in the U.S. with a higher concentration of residence and rural customers than the Bell System itself.

Inter-LATA: Services, revenues, functions, etc., that relate to telecommunications originating in one Local Access and Transport Area (LATA) and terminating in another LATA or outside of a LATA.

Intra-LATA: Services, revenues, functions, etc., that relate to telecommunications originating and terminating within a single Local Access and Transport Area (LATA).

Local Access and Transport Area (LATA): The term "exchange" is defined in the Modification of Final Judgment (MFJ) as new areas established by the Bell Operating telephone companies (BOCs) to encompass areas of "common social, economic, and other purposes," for the purpose of defining the territory within which a BOC may offer its exchange telecommunications and exchange-access services. To avoid confusing these new areas with existing exchanges, AT&T has labeled the proposed limiting boundary of BOC operations as local access and transport areas (LATAs).

Local loop: The channel or circuit that goes from the customer's premises to the serving central office. Part of the "joint" plant.

Local measured service (LMS): A method of pricing local usage based on the number of local messages, the length of these messages, the time of day and the distance within the local exchange area. The purpose of local measured service is to charge customers an amount more in line with their actual usage.

National Exchange Carrier Association (NECA): The access-charge plan mandated the establishment of a NECA to collect and pay out the carrier's part of the charges for access to non–traffic-sensitive plant, instead of requiring all exchange carriers to pool uniform charges. The NECA also files tariffs and administers revenue pools for companies choosing to join in common tariffs for the other elements of access. AT&T was instructed to prepare and submit the initial associated tariffs, in view of the tight timetable for divestiture.

Natural monopoly: An economic concept that recognizes that one firm can provide certain services (such as telecommunications) more economically and efficiently than can two or more firms competing to provide these services.

Other common carrier (OCC): Includes specialized common carriers (SCCs), domestic and International Record Carriers (IRCs) and domestic satellite carriers that are authorized by the FCC to provide communications services in competition with the established telephone common carriers.

Point of presence (POP): A physical location within a Local Access and Transport Area (LATA) carrier establishes itself for the purpose of obtaining LATA access and to which the Bell Operating Company (BOC) provides access services.

Presubscription: A Bell Operating Company–tariffed service that will permit each customer served from an equal-access end-office switching system to route automatically, without the use of access codes, all the customer's inter-LATA communications to one inter-LATA carrier (IC) of the customer's choice.

Rate base: The total invested capital, net of disallowances, upon which a regulated telephone company is allowed to earn a rate of return.

Rate of return: The resultant post-tax earnings that are generated from business operations, before interest deductions, related to the debt and equity capital obligations. The term is also used at times to describe the ratio of return (net income before interest deduction) to the rate base.

Separations: The process by which telephone property costs, revenues, expenses, taxes and reserves are assigned between interstate operations, subject to the jurisdiction of the FCC, and the intrastate operations, subject to the jurisdiction of the several state regulatory bodies.

Settlements: Procedures established by the telephone common carriers for distributing joint interstate and intrastate revenues between Bell System and Independent Telephone Companies after reimbursement of expenses, in proportion to their investment.

Standard metropolitan statistical area (SMSA): A geographical area defined by the U.S. Office of Management and Budget for the gathering and reporting of federal statistics. The general concept is one of a large population center, together with adjacent communities that have a high degree of economic and social integration with that center. SMSA boundaries are used as reference points when defining exchange areas in the Modification of Final Judgement (MFJ).

Terminal equipment: Any device which terminates a communications channel and adapts that channel for use by a user, the user being either a person or a machine. Telephone sets, switchboards, data sets, teletypewriters, answering sets, etc., are examples of terminal equipment.

Index

133

About the Telecommunications Research and Action Center

The Telecommunications Research and Action Center (formerly the National Citizens Committee for Broadcasting) is a nonprofit, tax-exempt organization devoted to promoting the interests of consumers in the electronic media. TRAC works to enhance the rights of "electronic free speech" each of us hold as citizens and also strives to increase consumer access to traditional media as well as to the new communications technology.

Now in its 17th year of activity, TRAC is the oldest and the largest media reform organization in the United States. It is active in all phases of the electronic media, from radio and television to cable TV, and from telephones to the new communications technologies of tomorrow.

TRAC publishes *ACCESS*, a monthly journal of telecommunications. *ACCESS* is the only publication that covers media issues from a public-interest perspective. TRAC also publishes numerous consumer handbooks and pamphlets to help educate citizens on how to protect their own interests in the media.

TRAC is funded through the tax-deductible contributions of its members and subscribers. Membership is $25 a year, which also includes a subscription to TRAC's quarterly newsletter Tele-Tips. To join TRAC, or for more information, write to TRAC, Box 12038, Washington, DC 20005; or call 202-462-2520.

About the Author

Samuel A. Simon is president of the Telecommunications Research and Action Center (TRAC), formerly the National Citizens Committee for Broadcasting. Mr. Simon is editor of *ACCESS* (the citizens journal of telecommunications) and the author of *Reverse the Charges: How to Save Money on Your Telephone Bill* and *Citizens Primer on The Fairness Doctrine.* He is active as a speaker and writer of many articles and reports.

Mr. Simon is an adjunct professor of law at New York Law School, and is also co-chair of Tele-Consumer Hotline, a national consumer information service. Previously, he was Senior Attorney for the Federal Trade Commission.

Related Titles from Knowledge Industry Publications, Inc.

The Future of Videotext: Worldwide Prospects for Home/Office Electronic Information Services
by Efrem Sigel, *et al.*
ISBN 0-86729-025-0   hardcover $34.95

The Birth of Electronic Publishing: Legal and Economic Issues in Telephone, Cable and Over-the-Air Teletext and Videotext
by Richard M. Neustadt
ISBN: 0-86729-030-7   hardcover $32.95

Protecting Privacy in Two-Way Electronic Services
by David H. Flaherty
ISBN: 0-86729-107-9   hardcover $34.95

Electronic Document Delivery: The Artemis Concept
by Adrian Norman
ISBN: 0-86729-011-0   hardcover $45.00

Electronic Marketing: Emerging TV and Computer Channels for Interactive Home Shopping
by Lawrence Strauss
ISBN: 0-86729-023-4   harcover $34.95

Information Technology: An Introduction
by Peter Zorkoczy
ISBN: 0-86729-037-4   hardcover $29.95

Guide to Electronic Publishing
by Fran Spigai and Peter Sommer
ISBN 0-914236-87-3   softcover $95.00

Available from Knowledge Industry Publications, Inc., 701 Westchester Ave., White Plains, NY 10604.